THE PICTURE BOOK OF

QUILTING

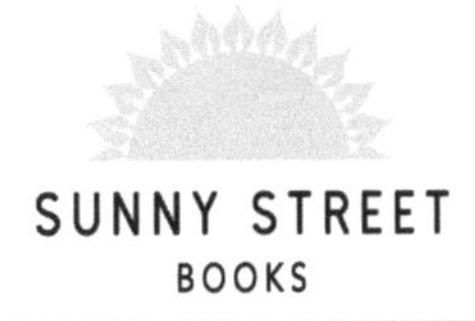

SUNNY STREET
BOOKS

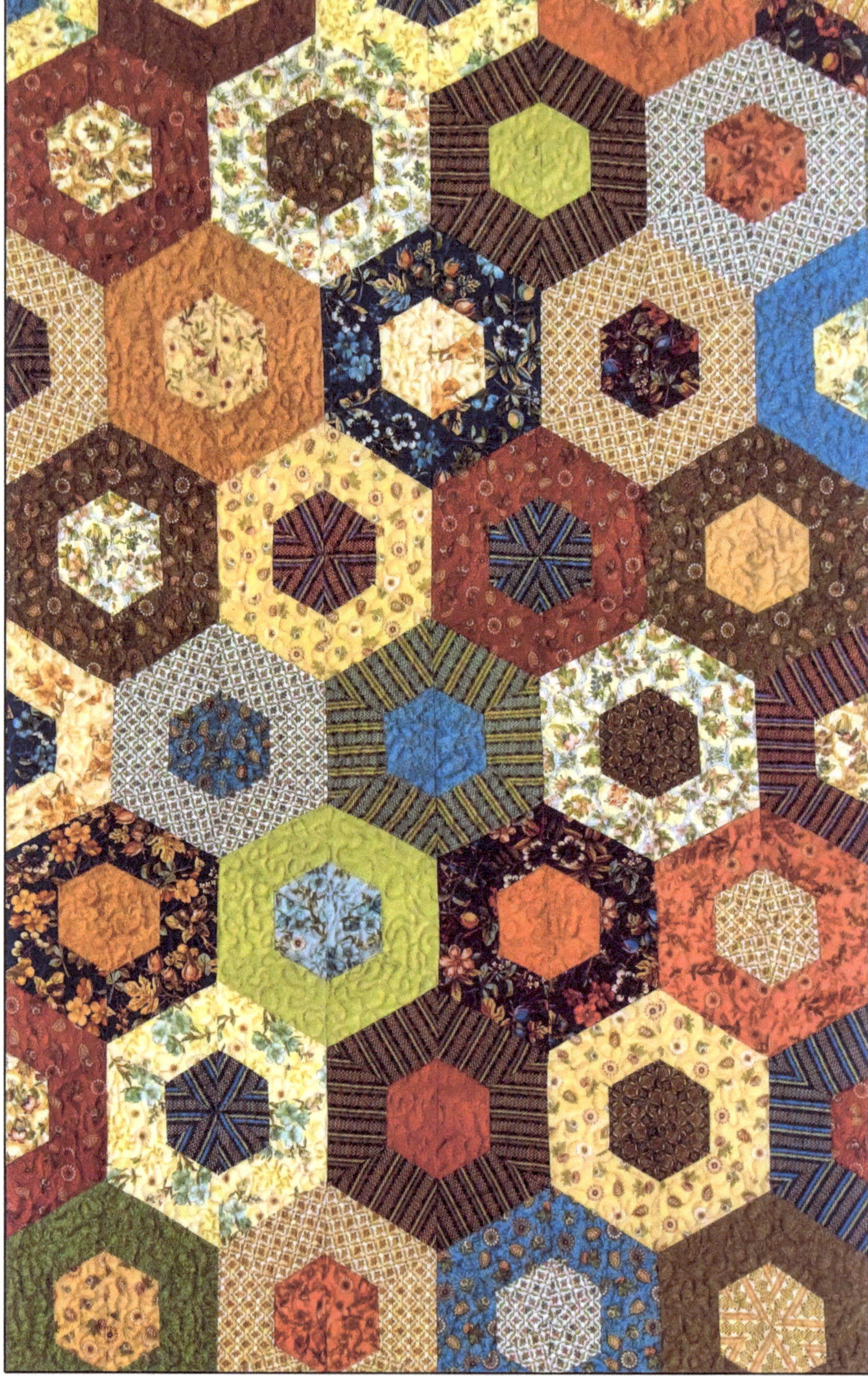

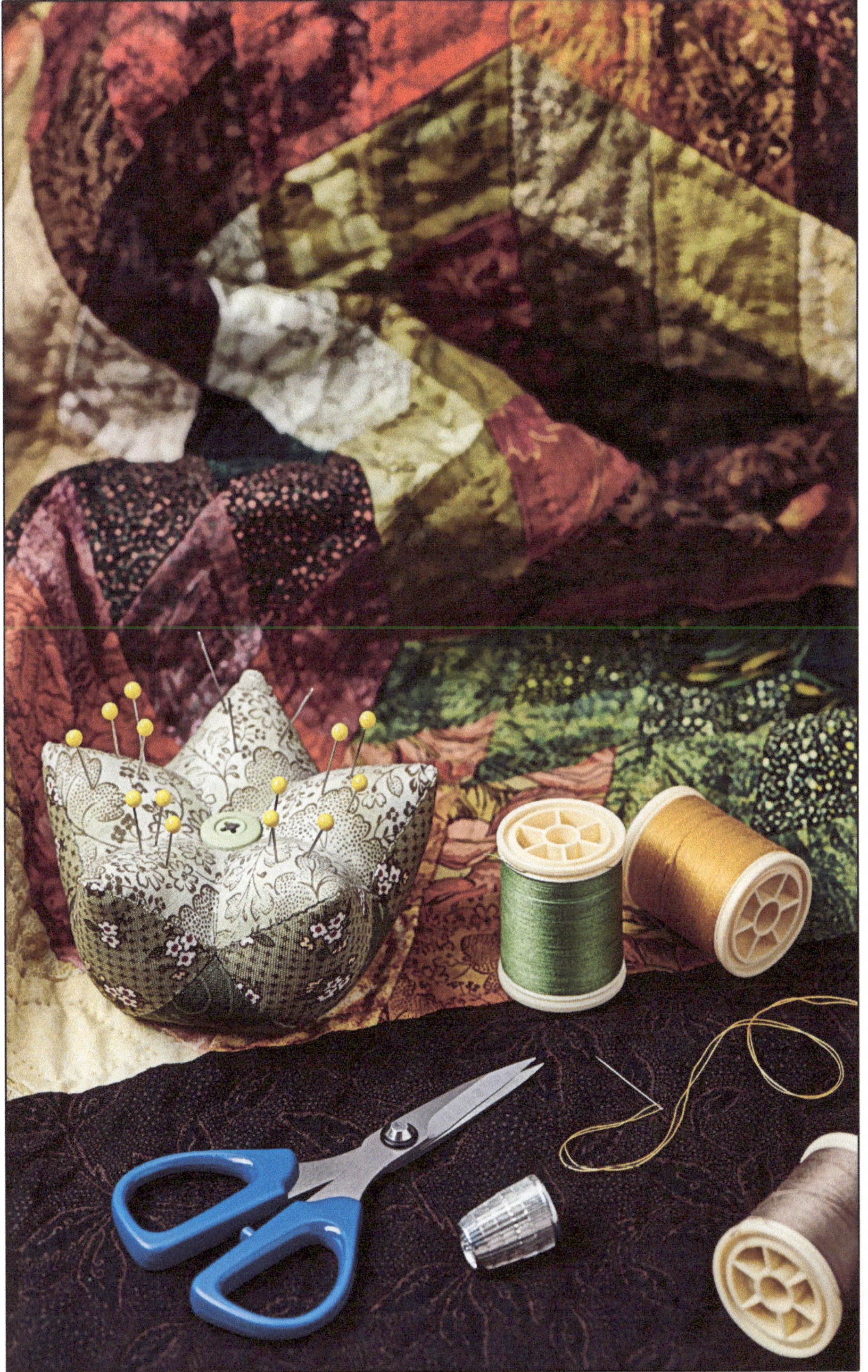

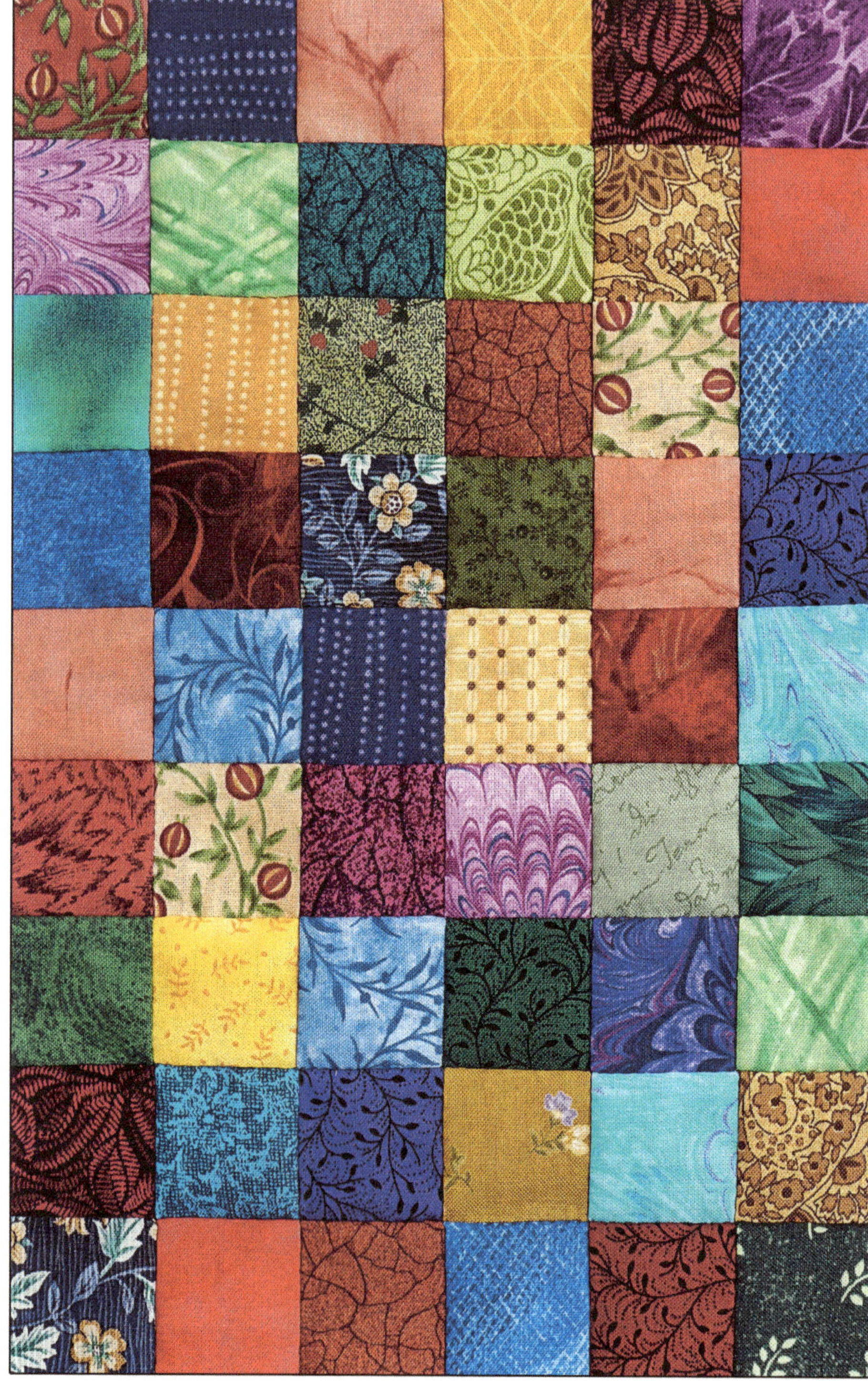

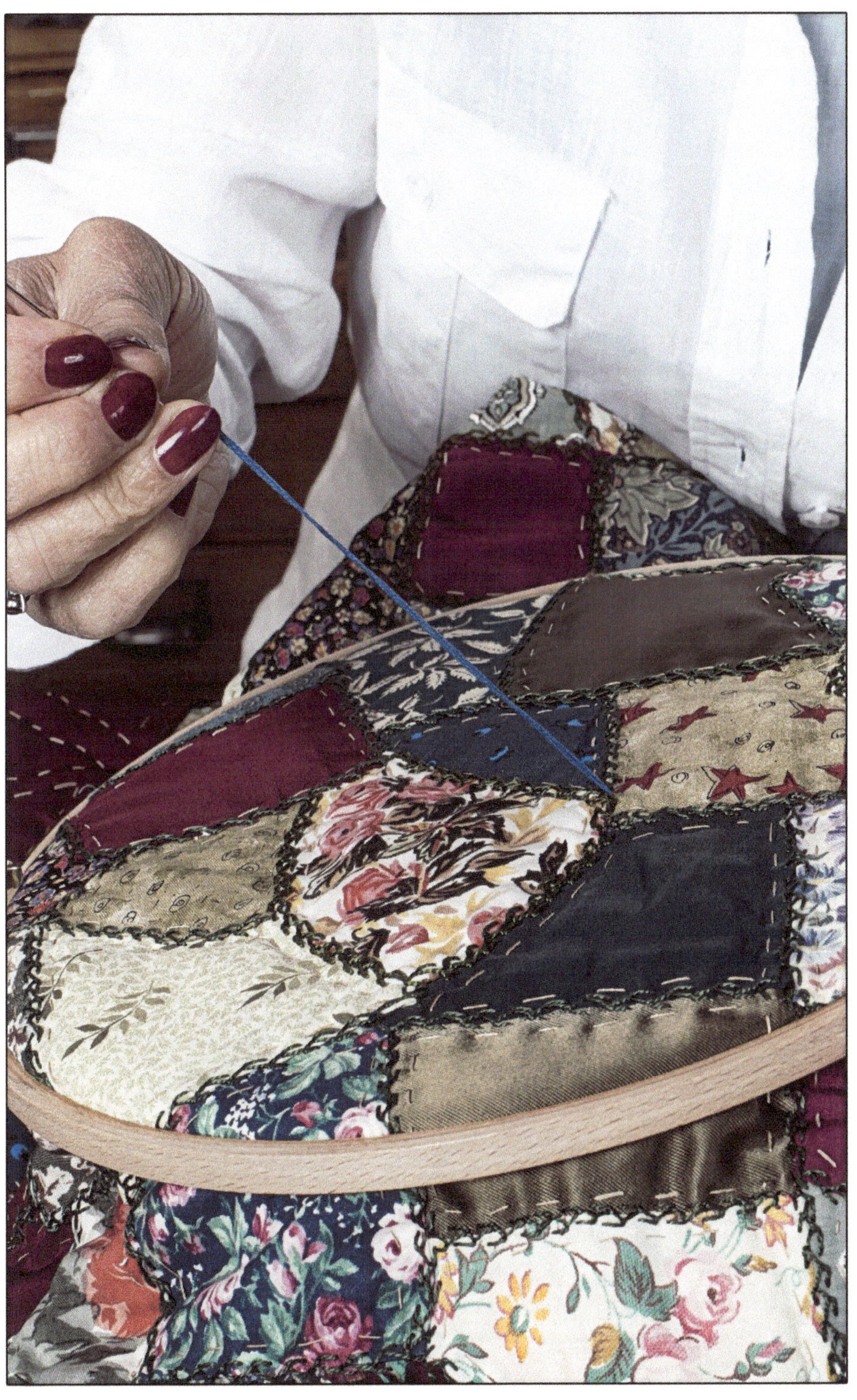

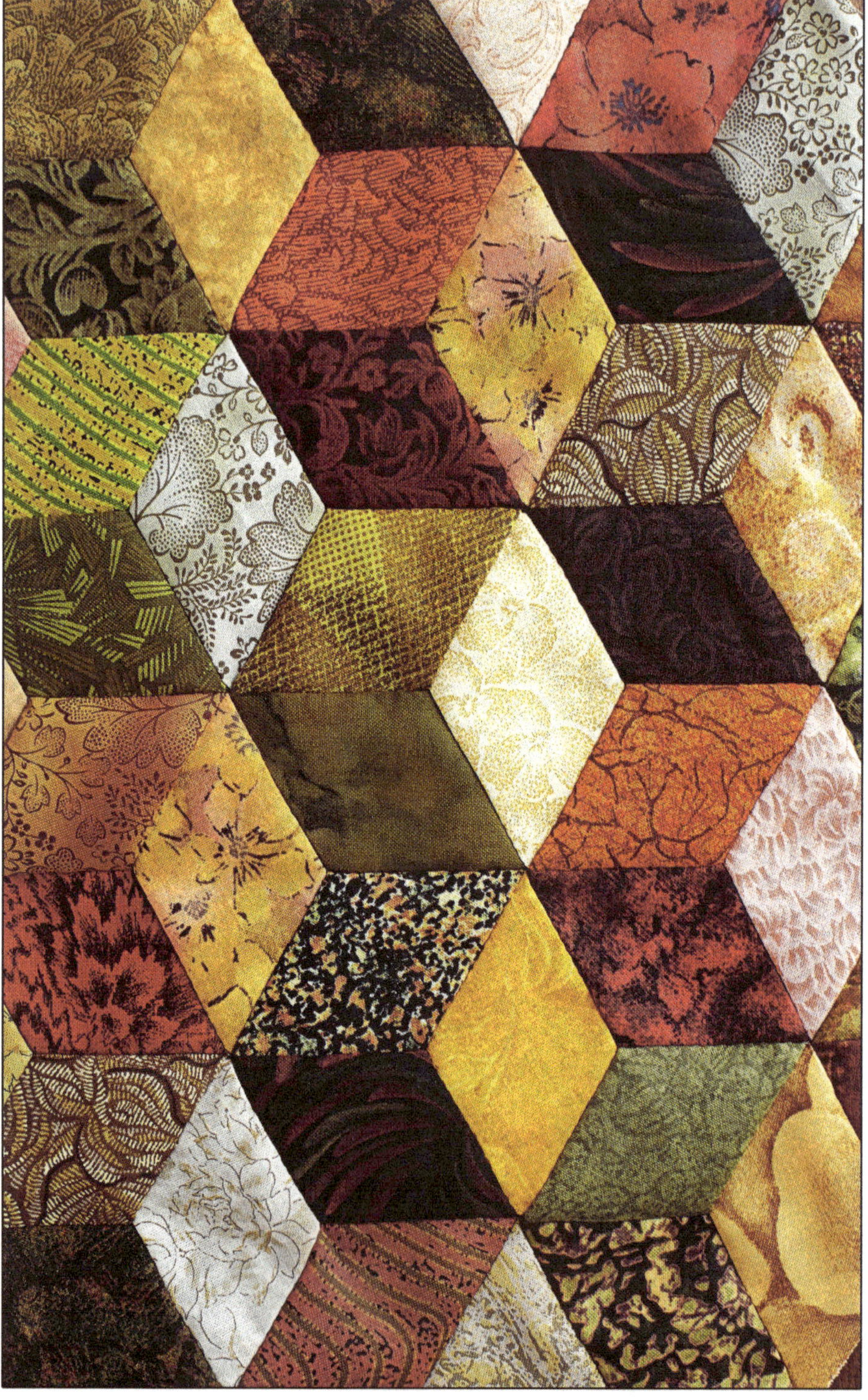

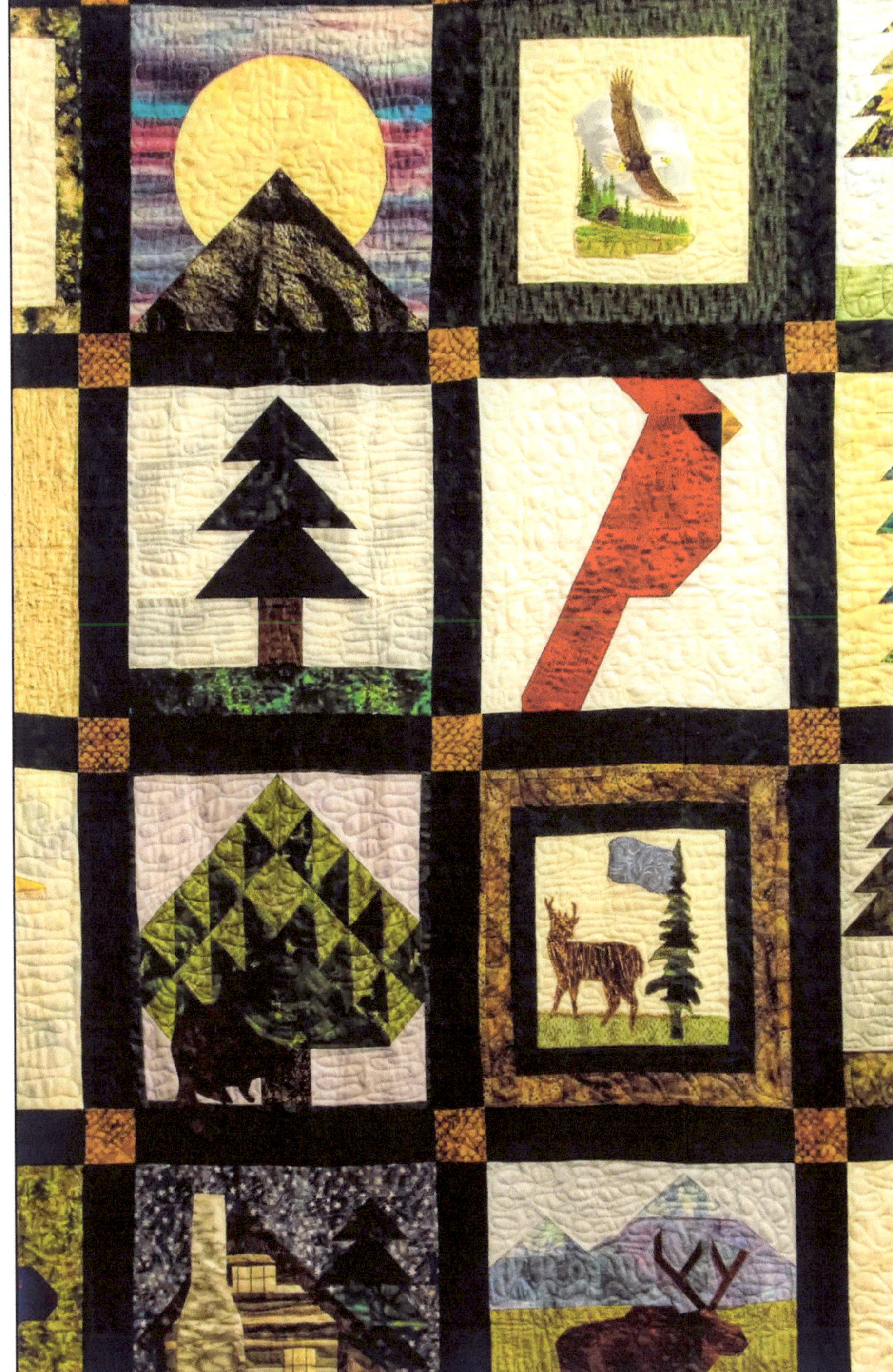

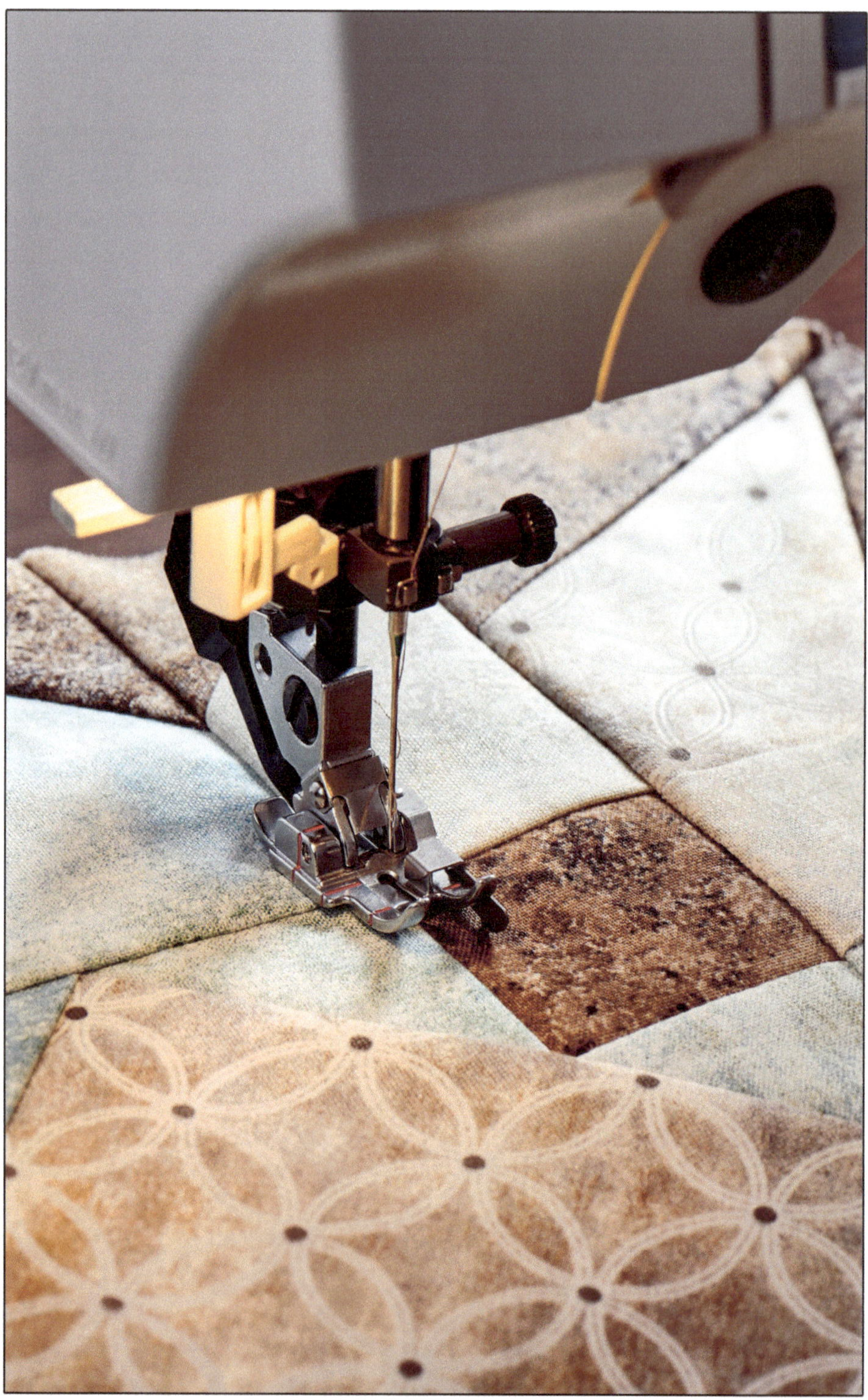

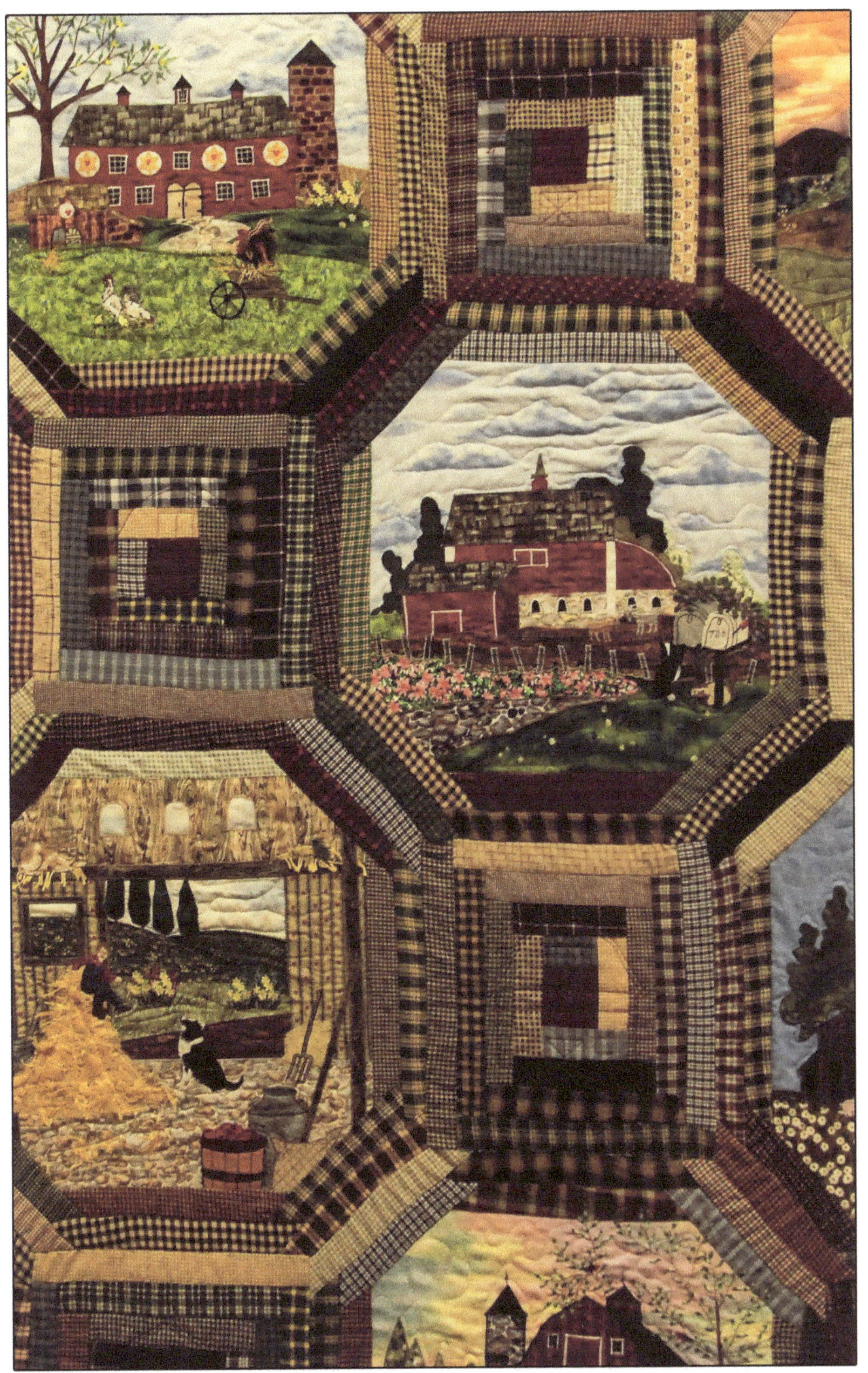

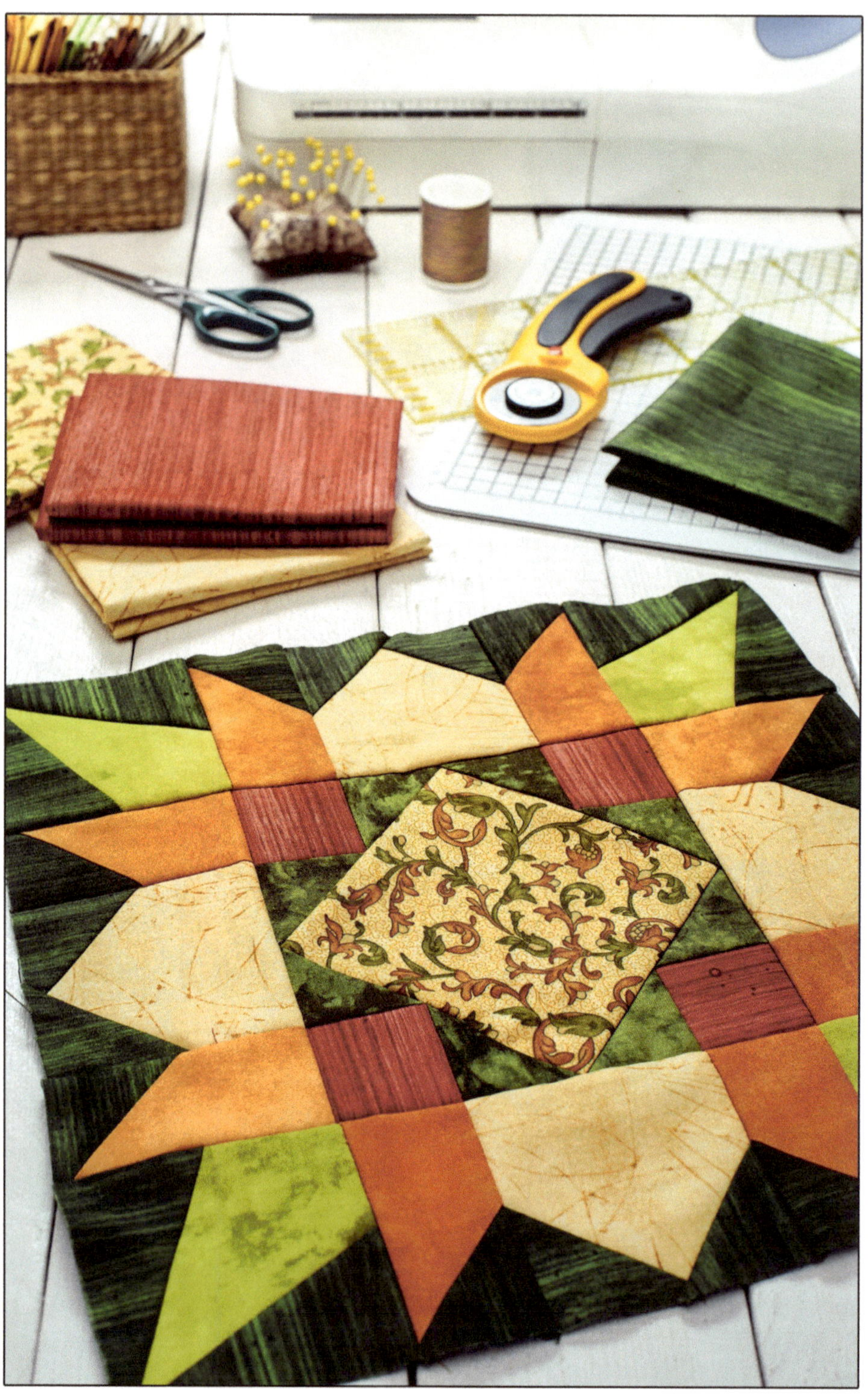

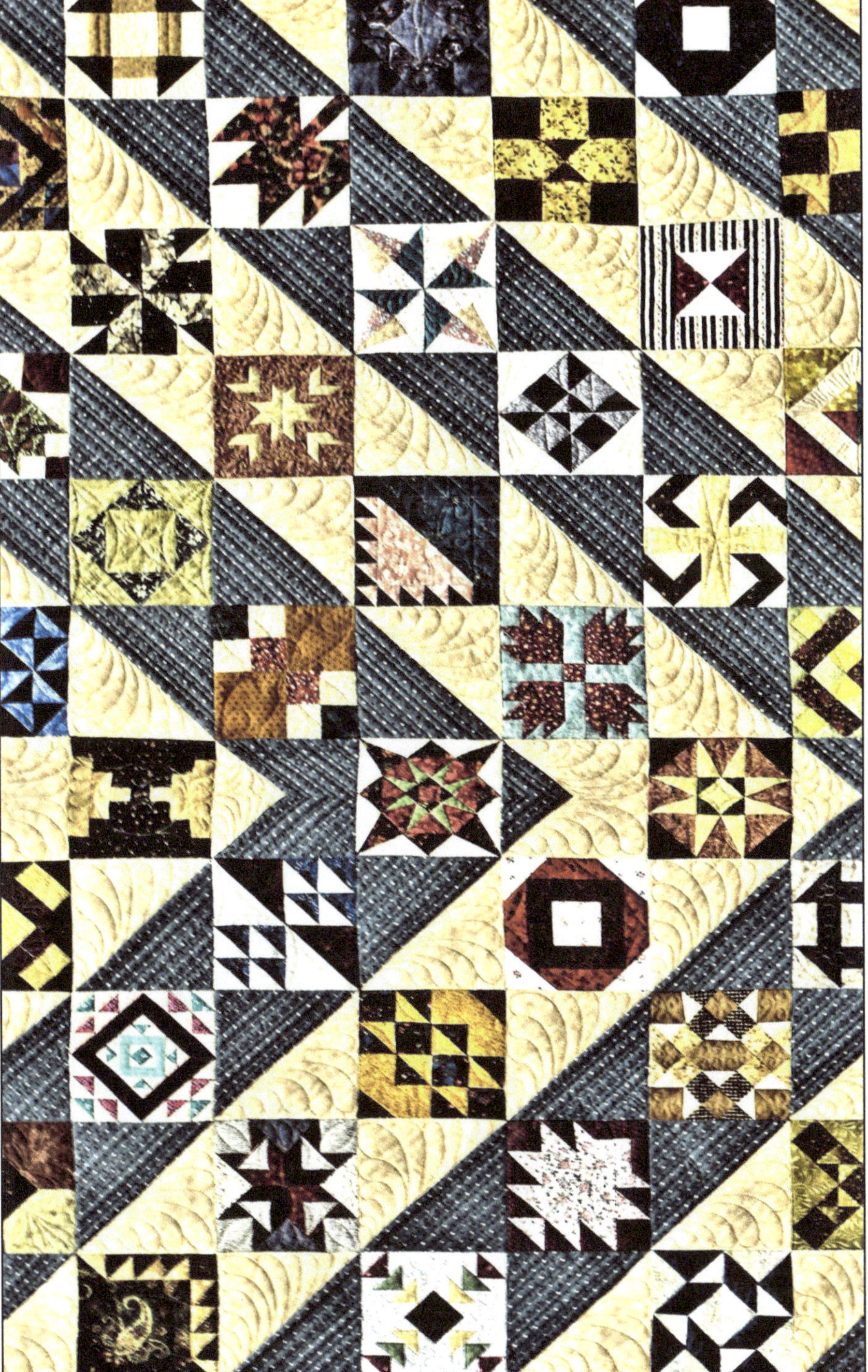

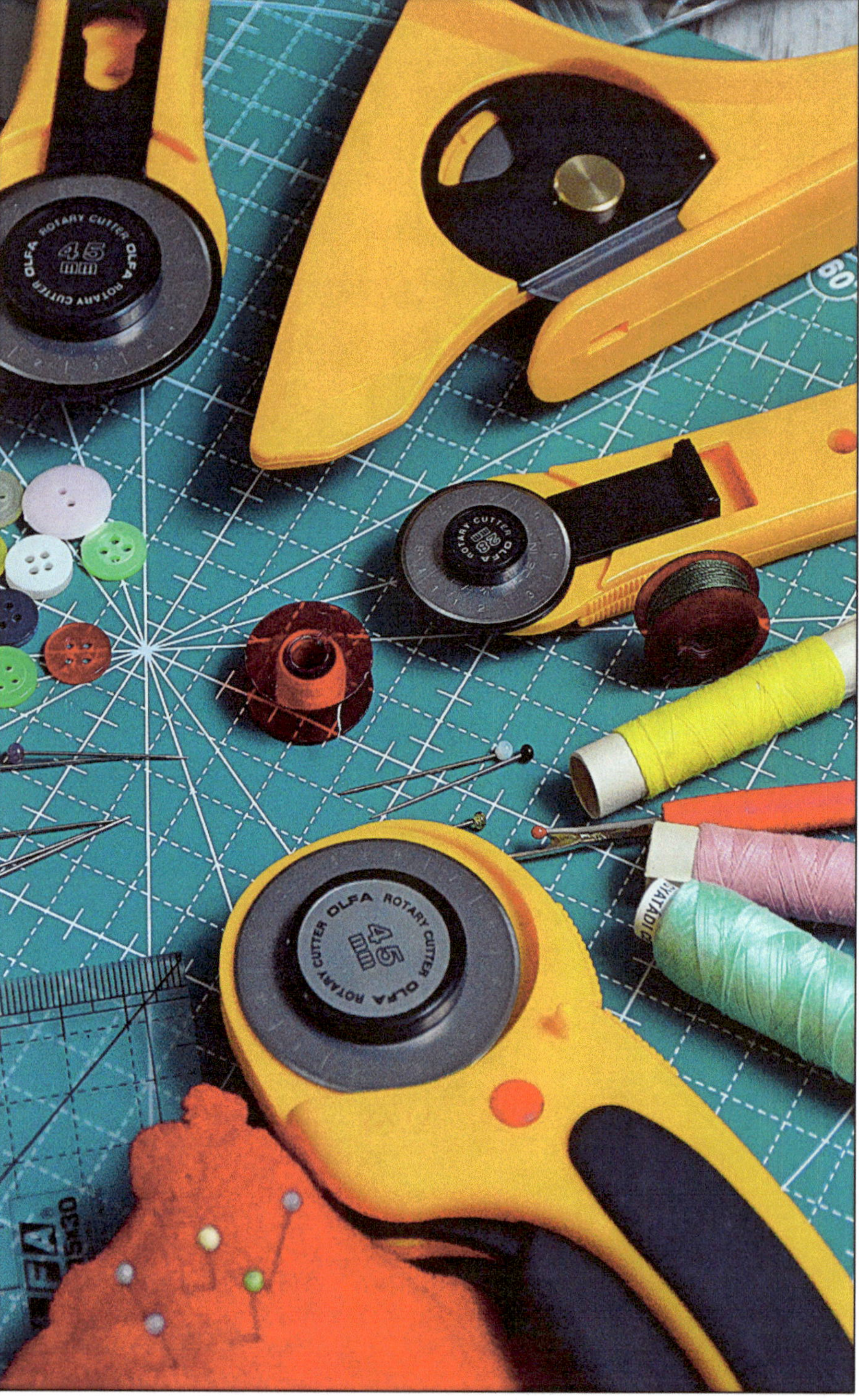

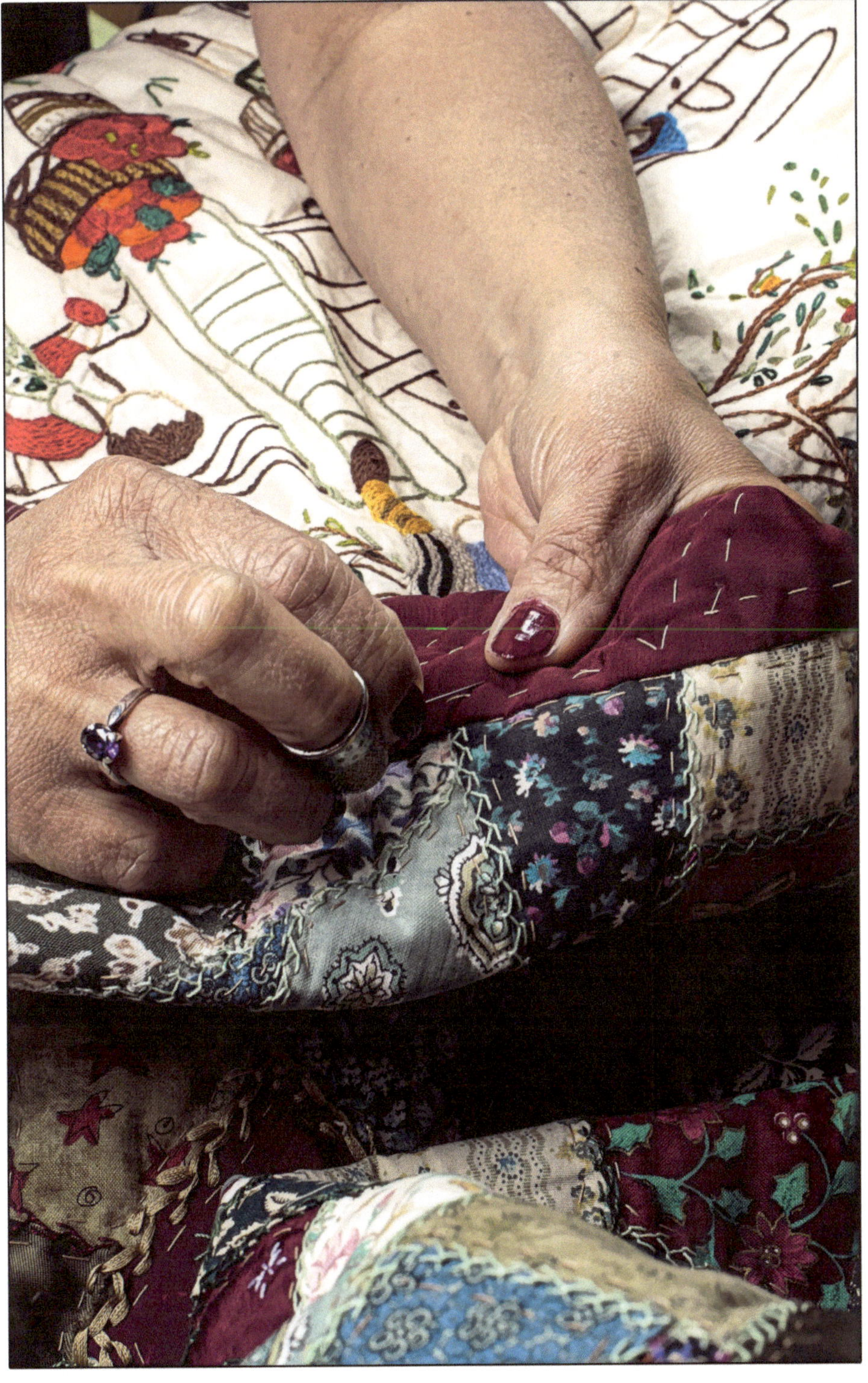

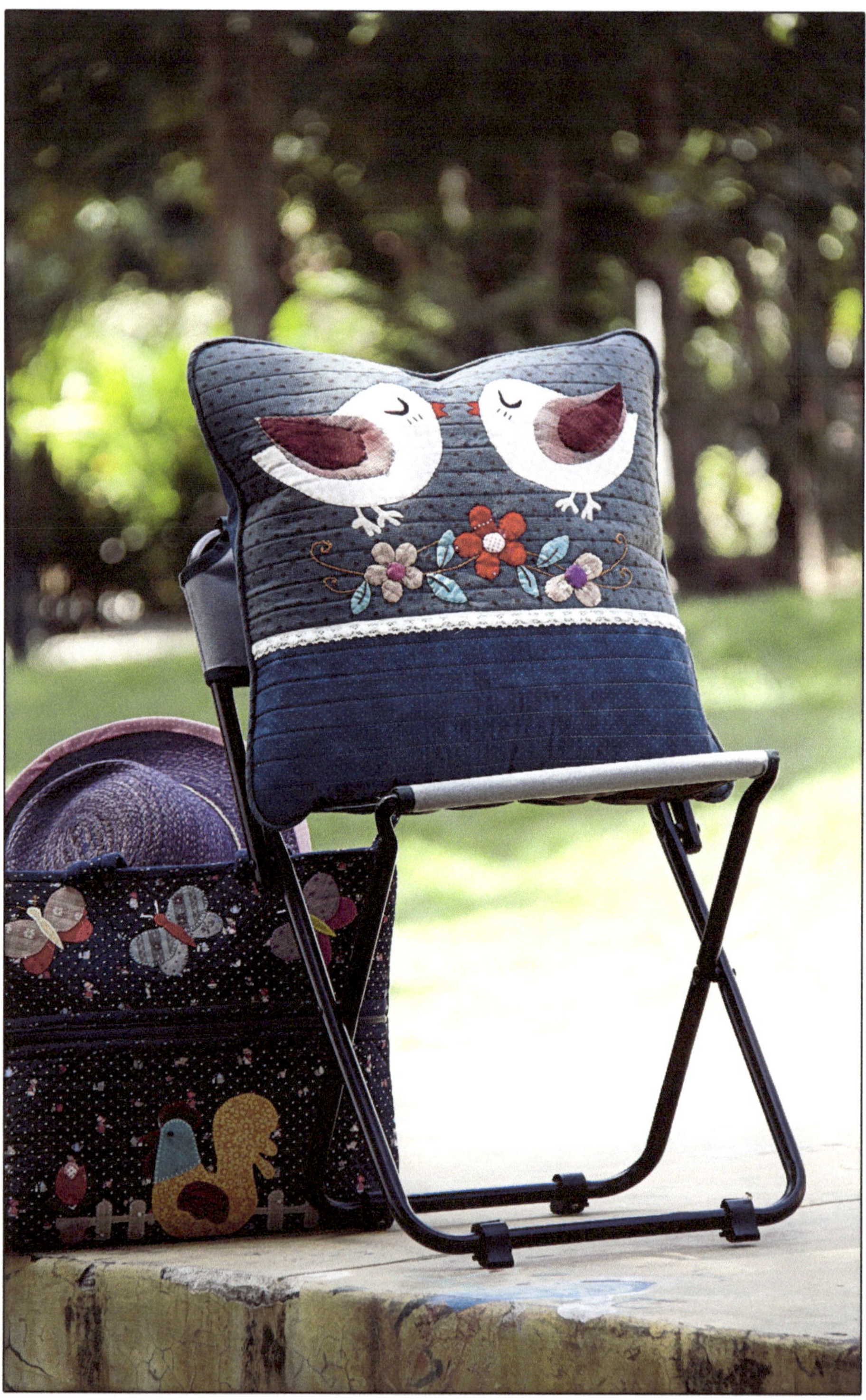

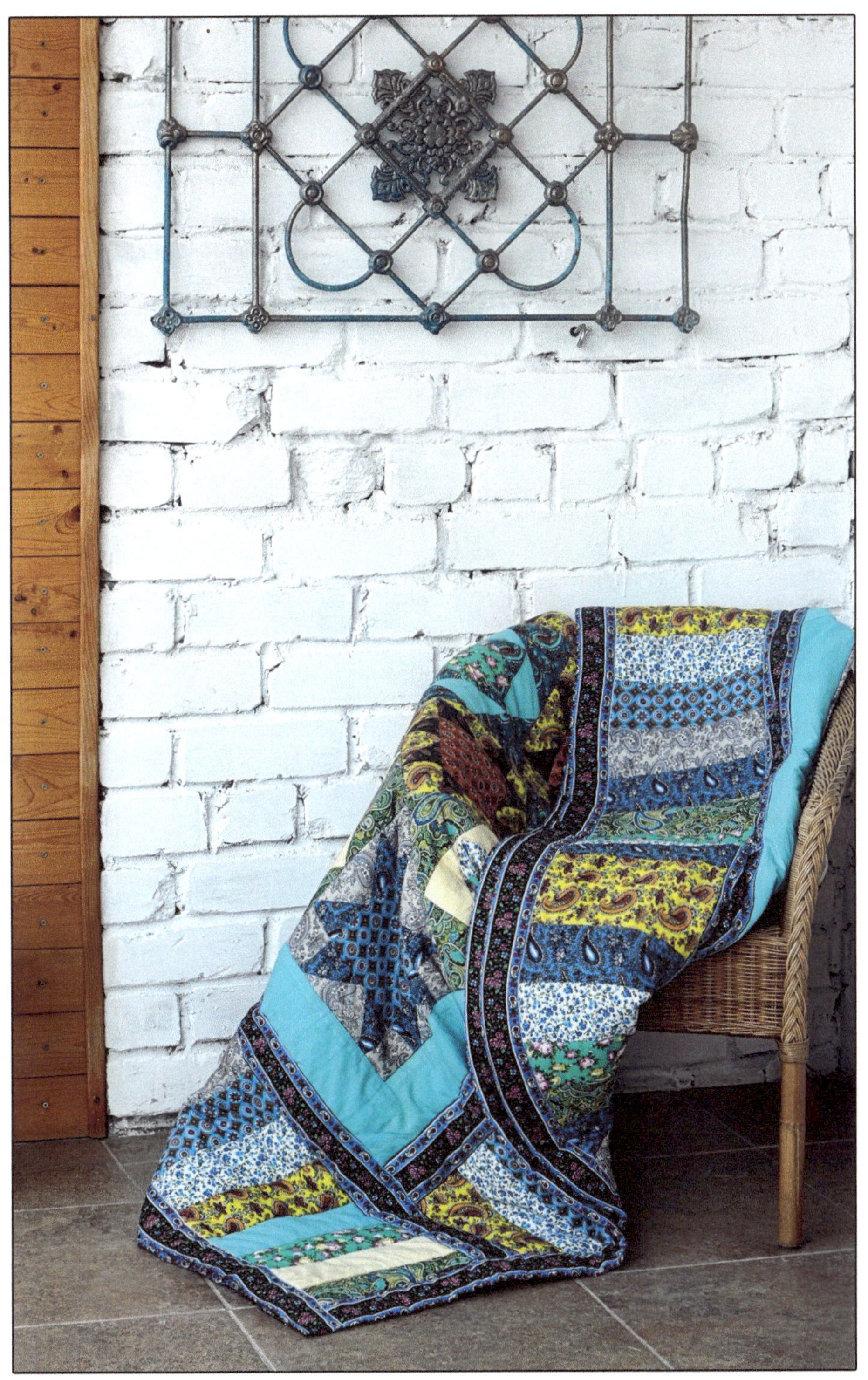

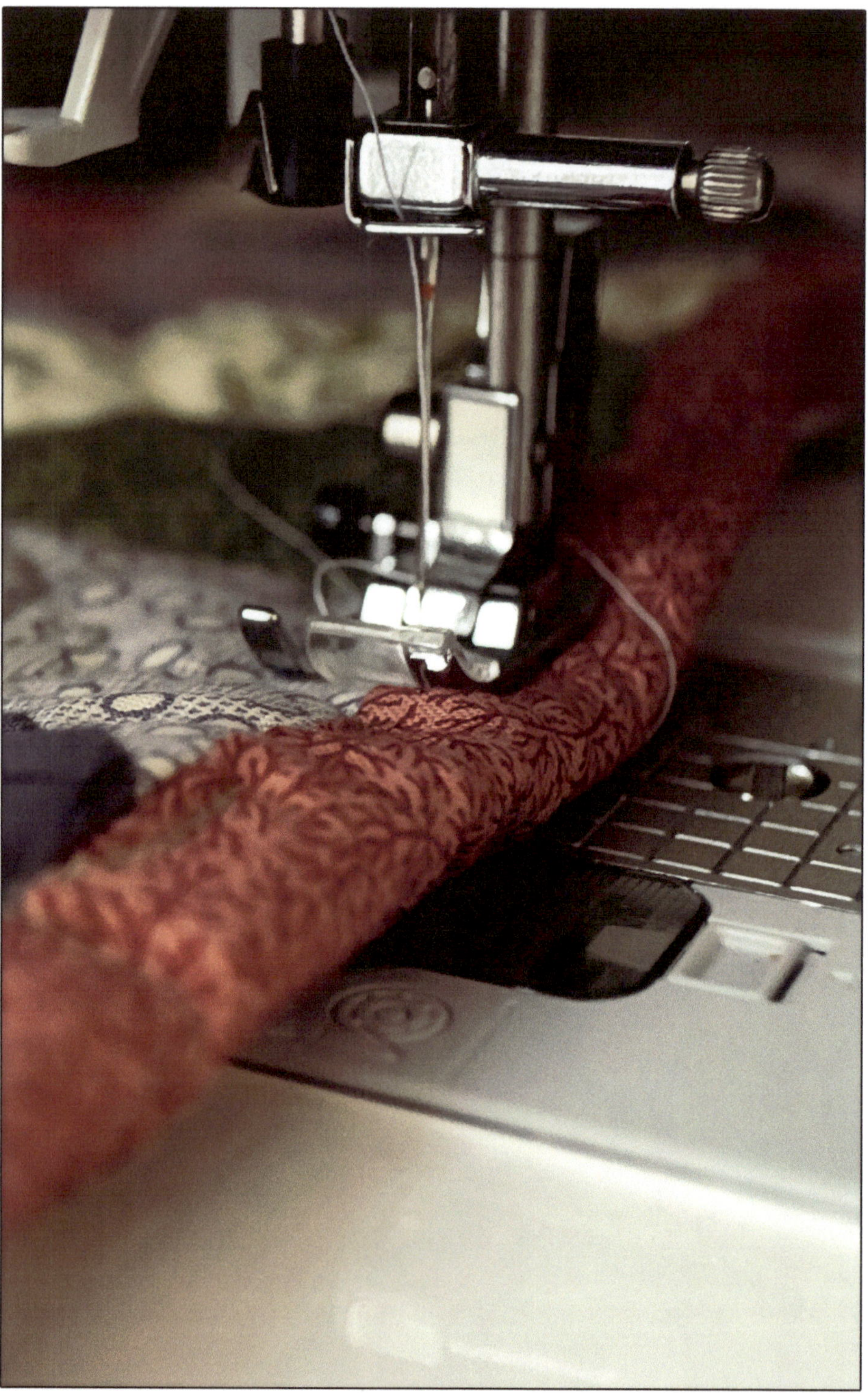

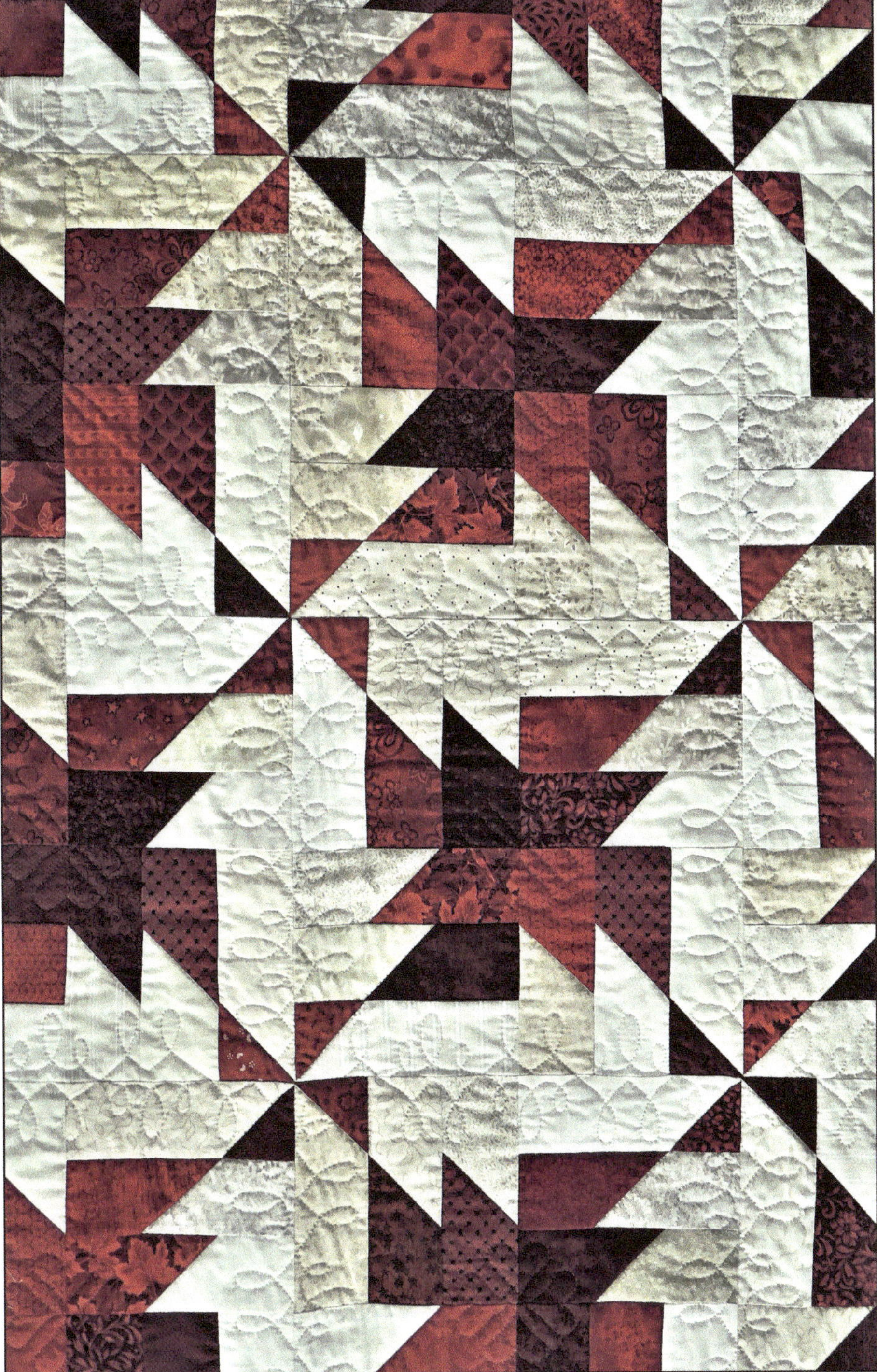

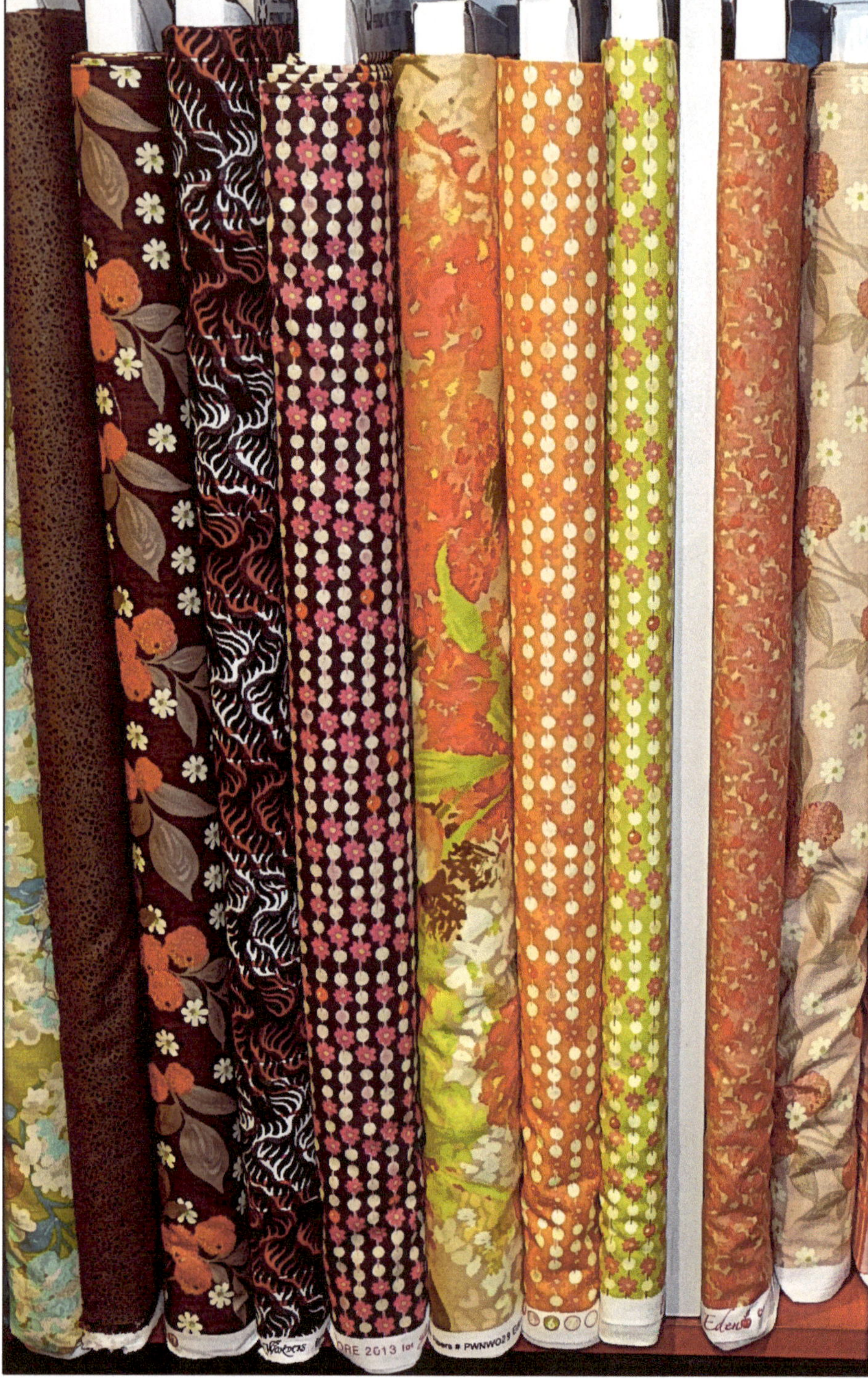

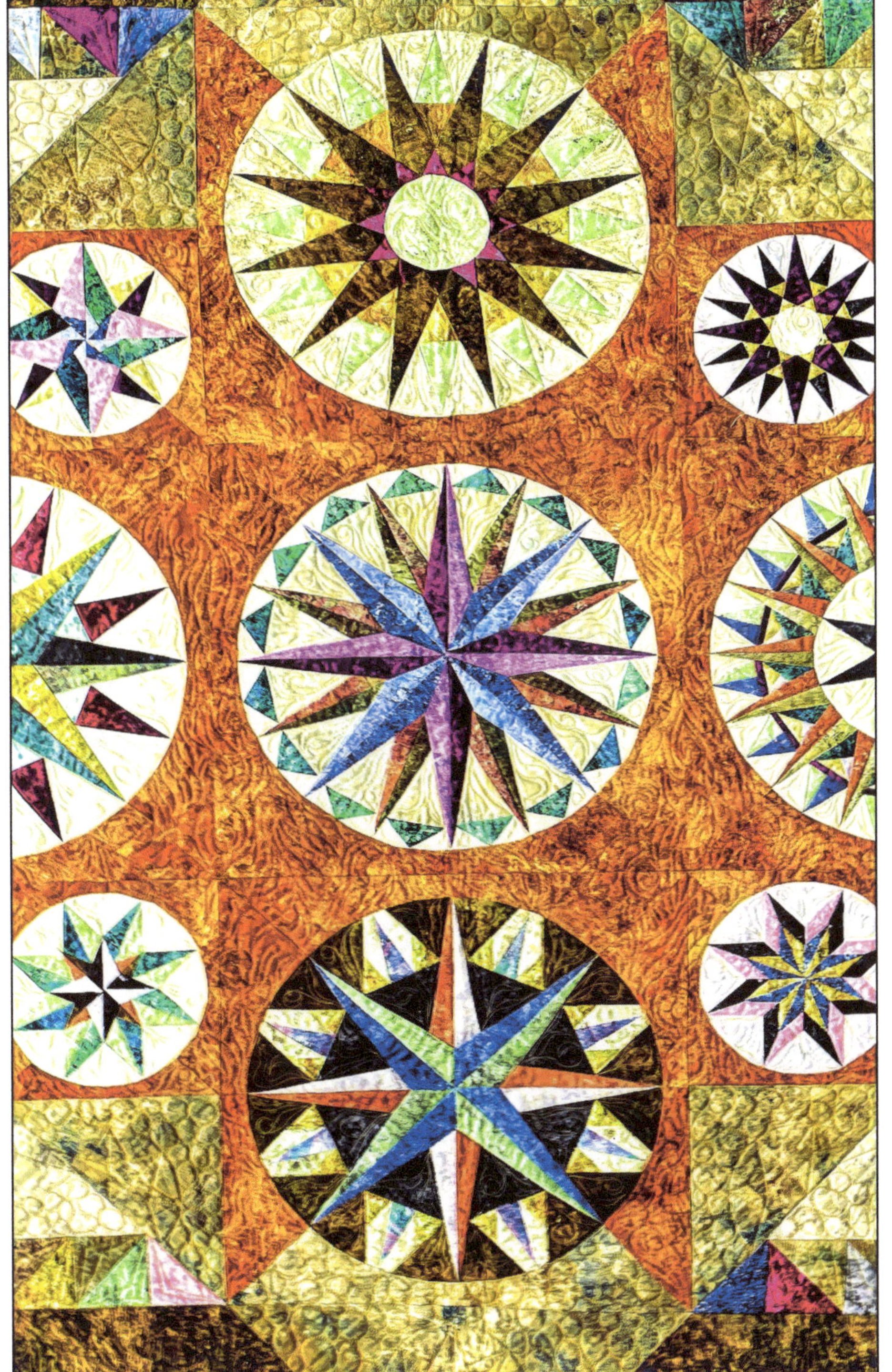

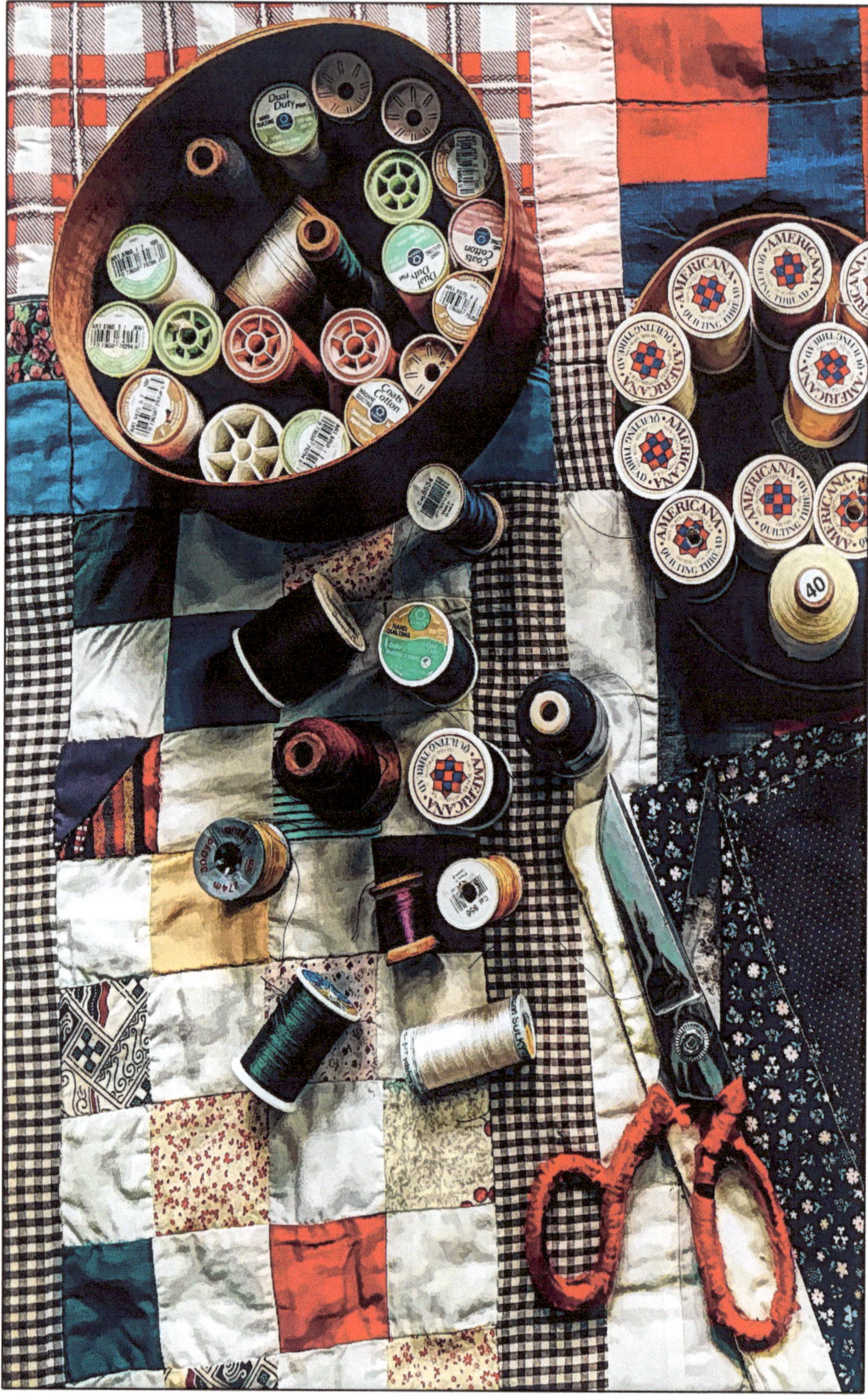

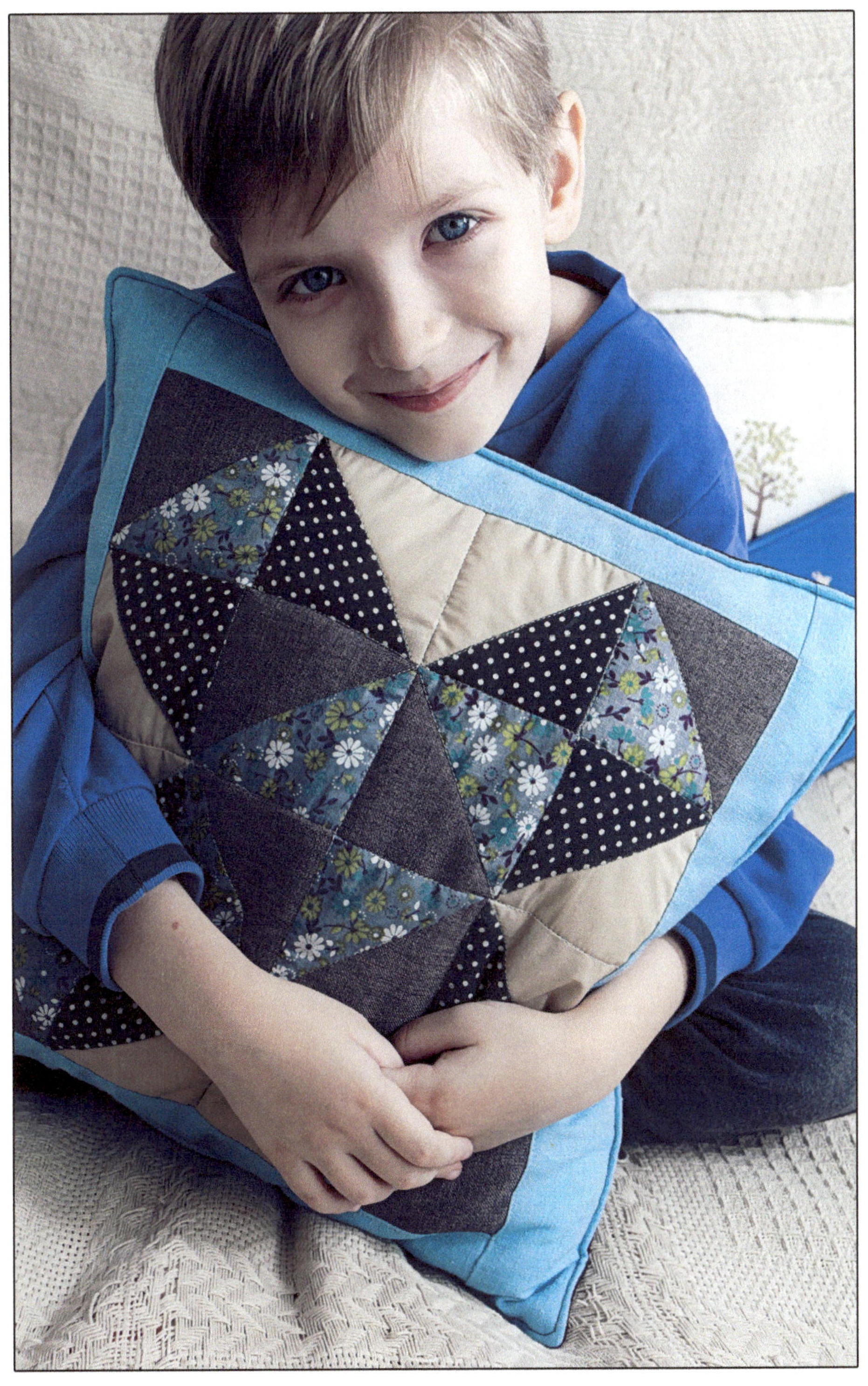

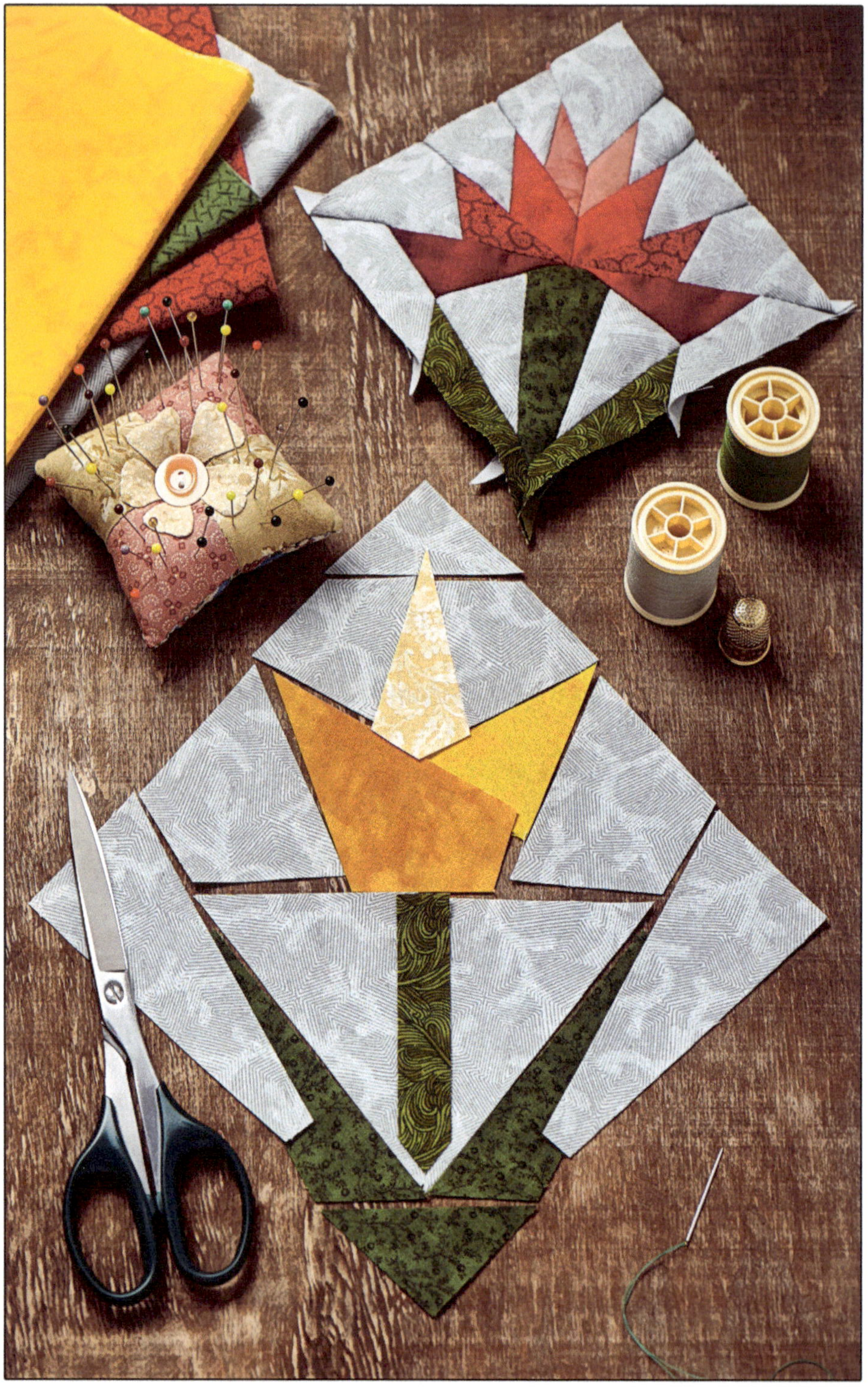

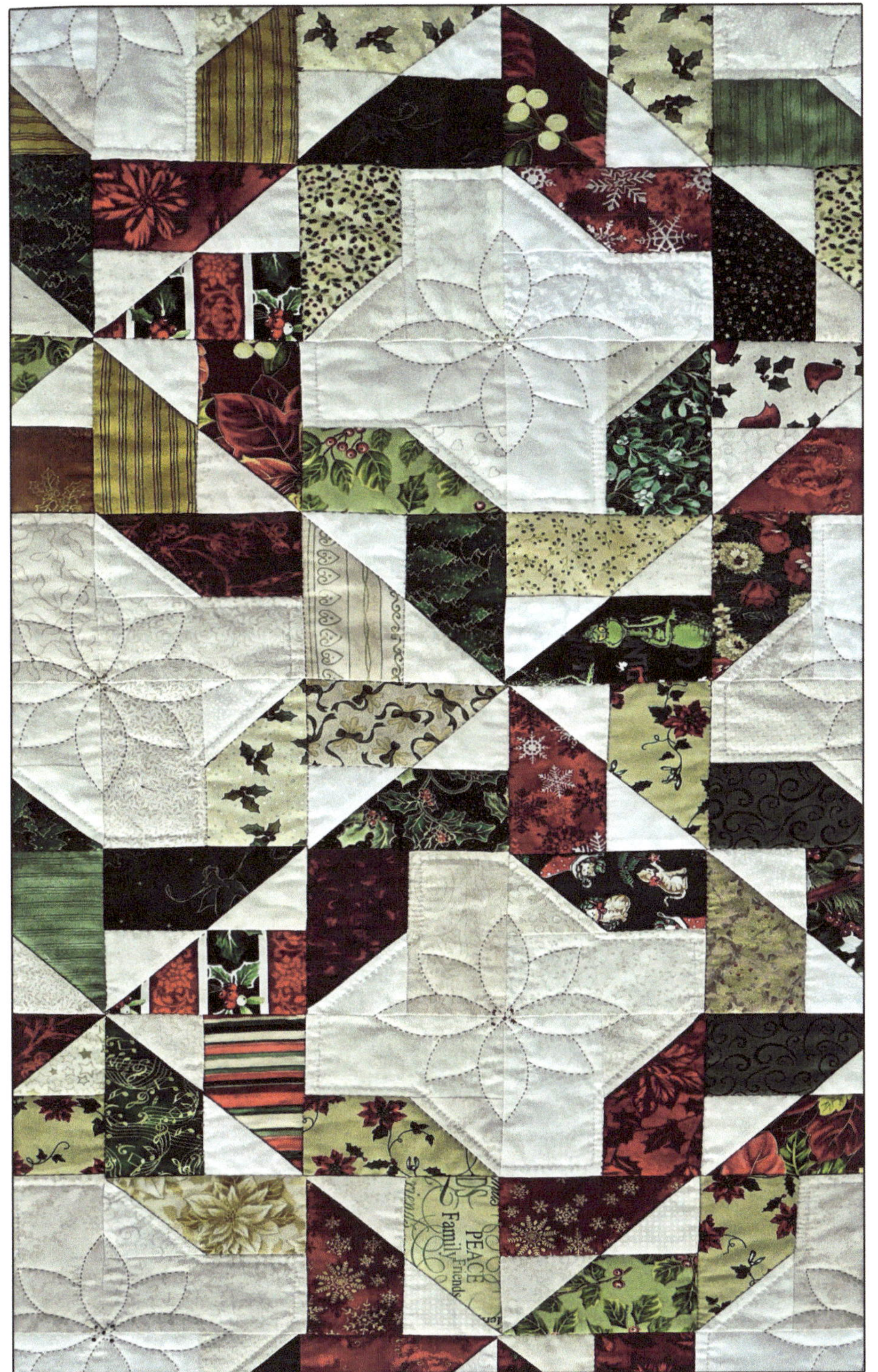

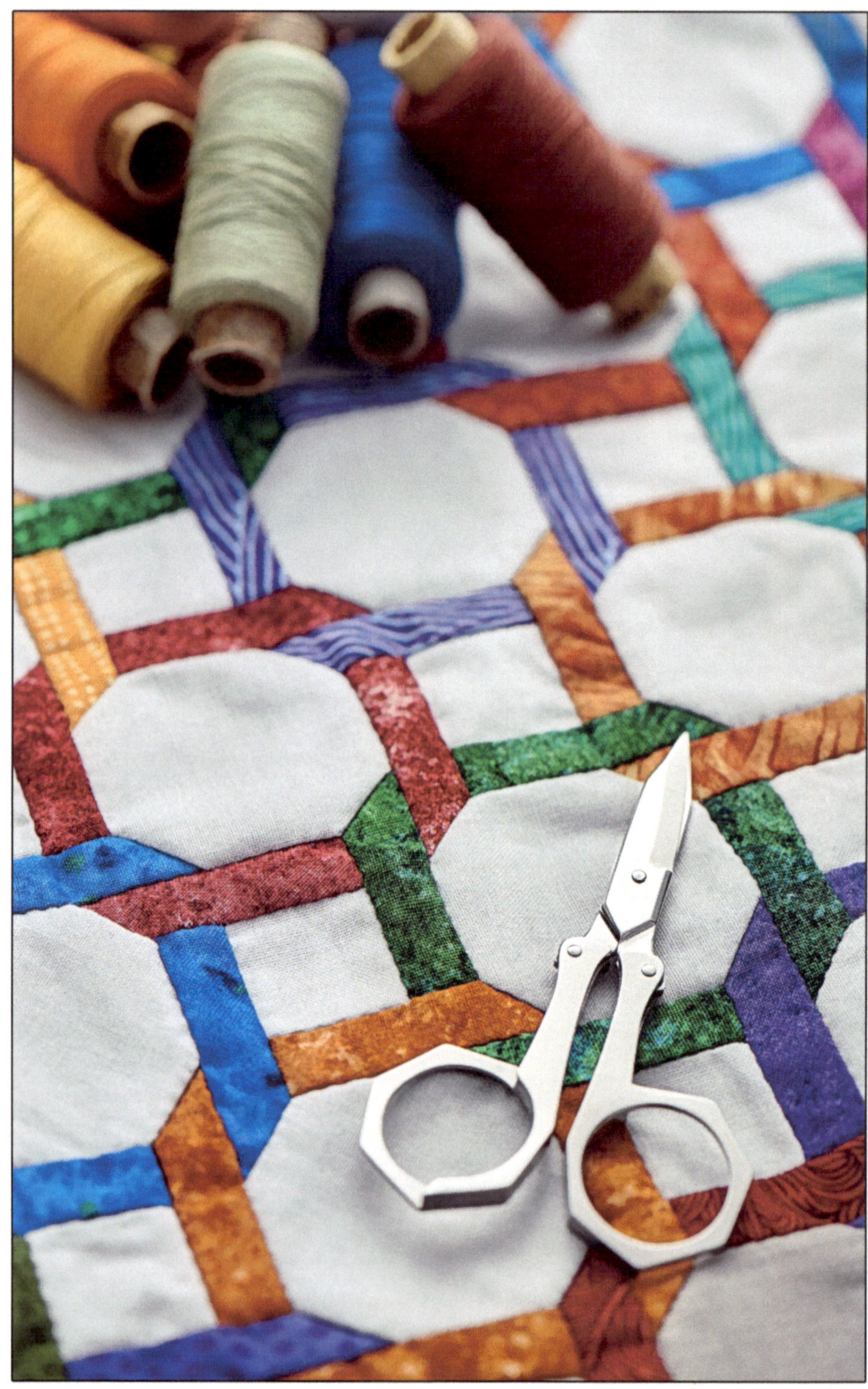

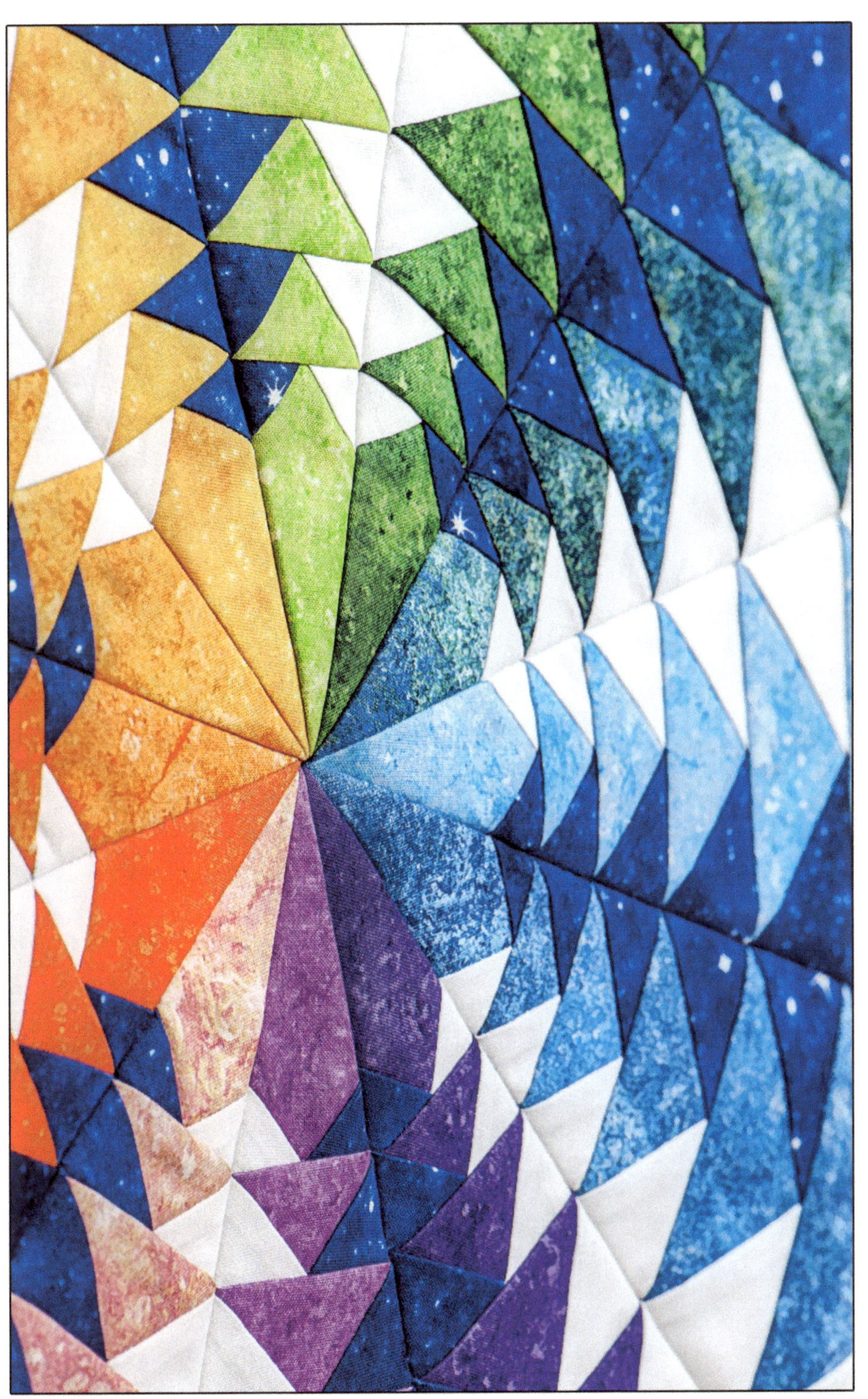

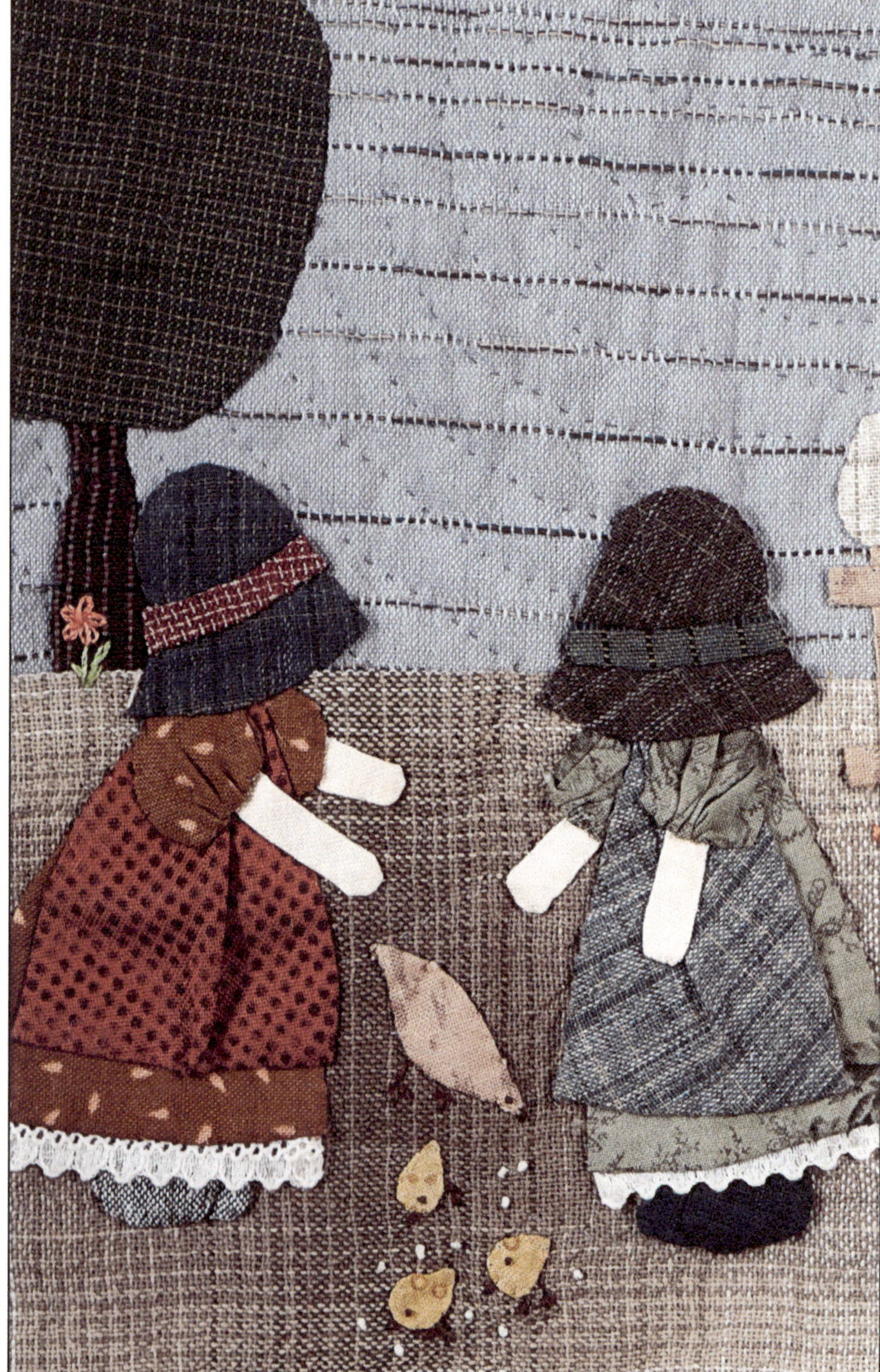

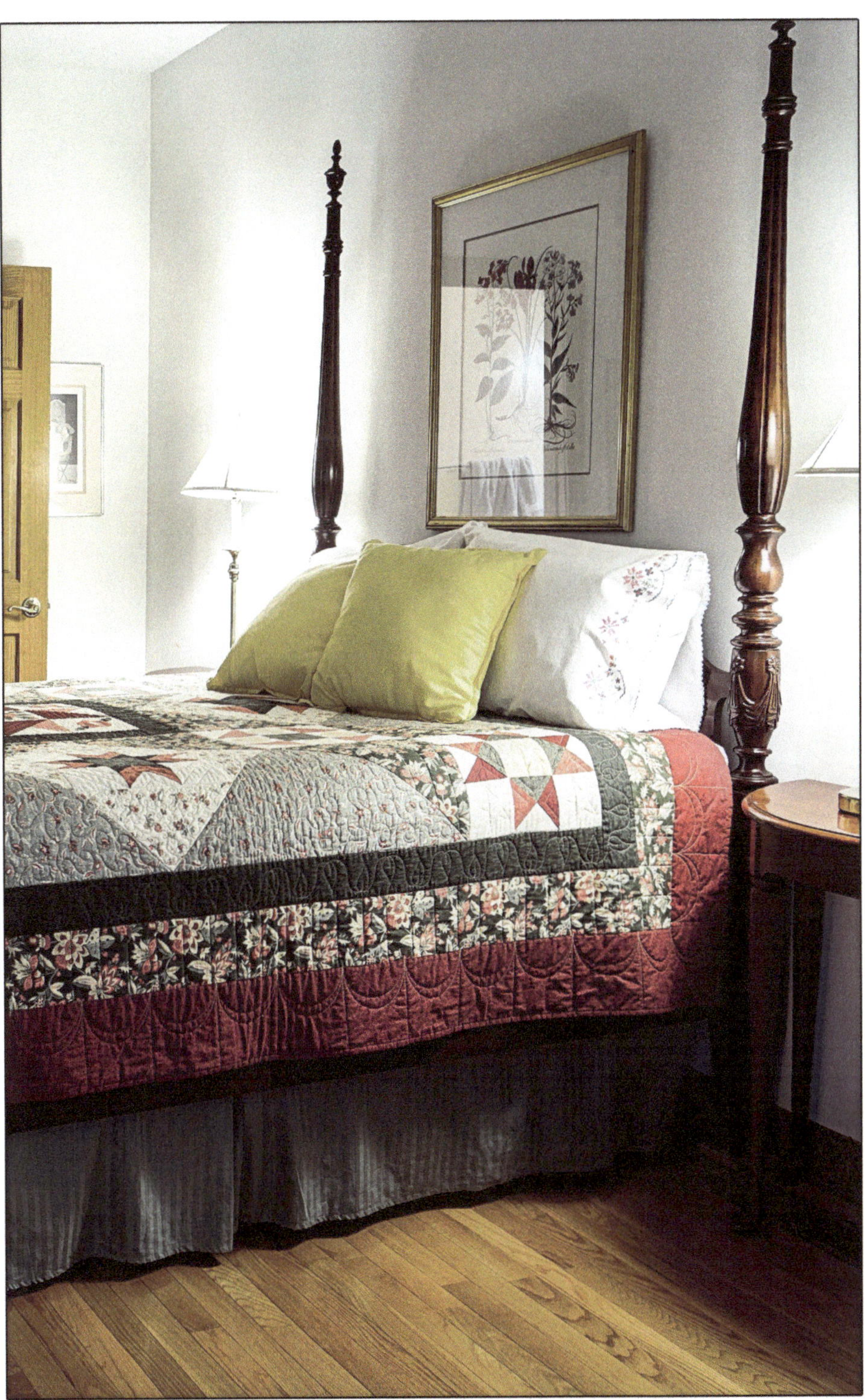

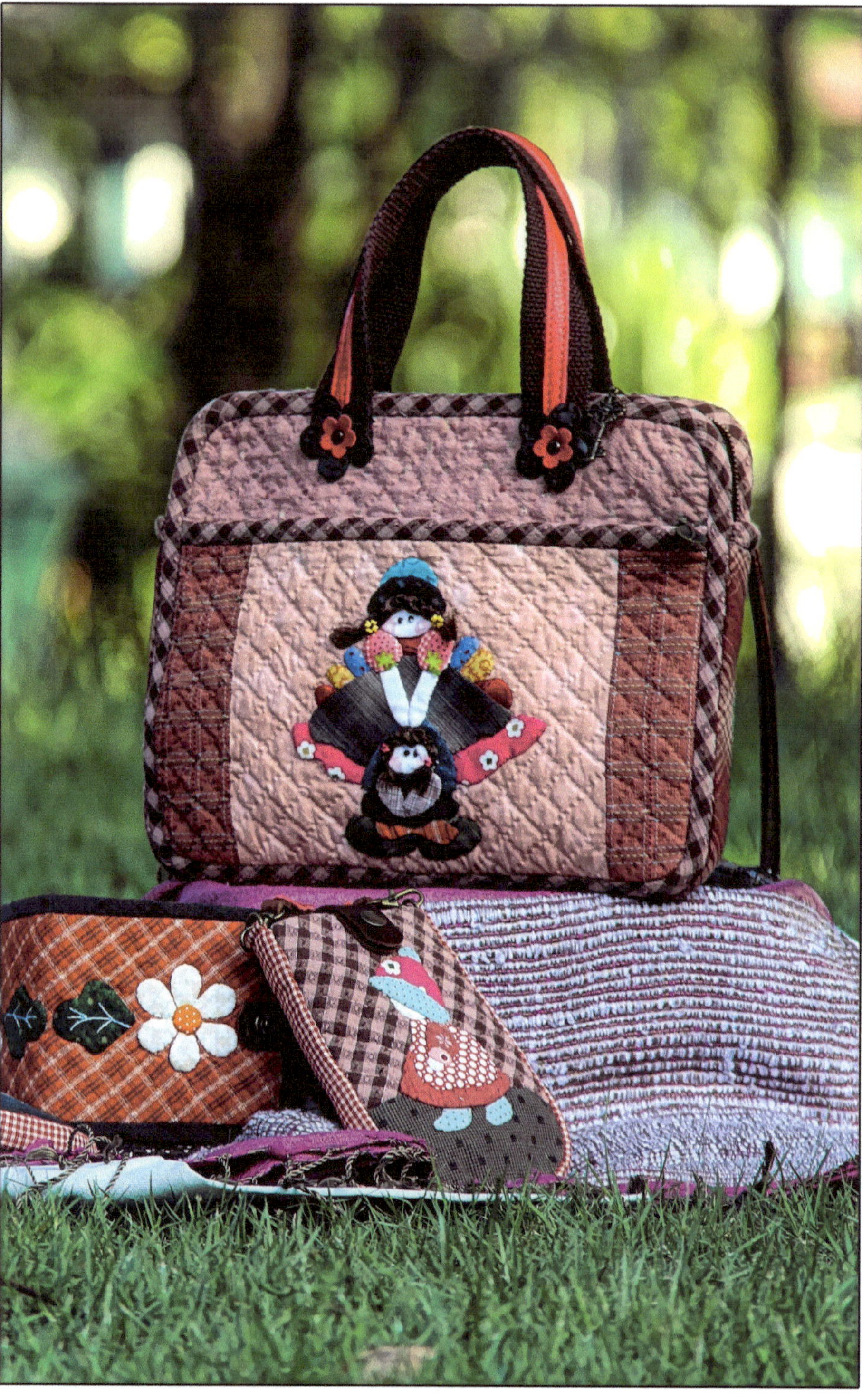

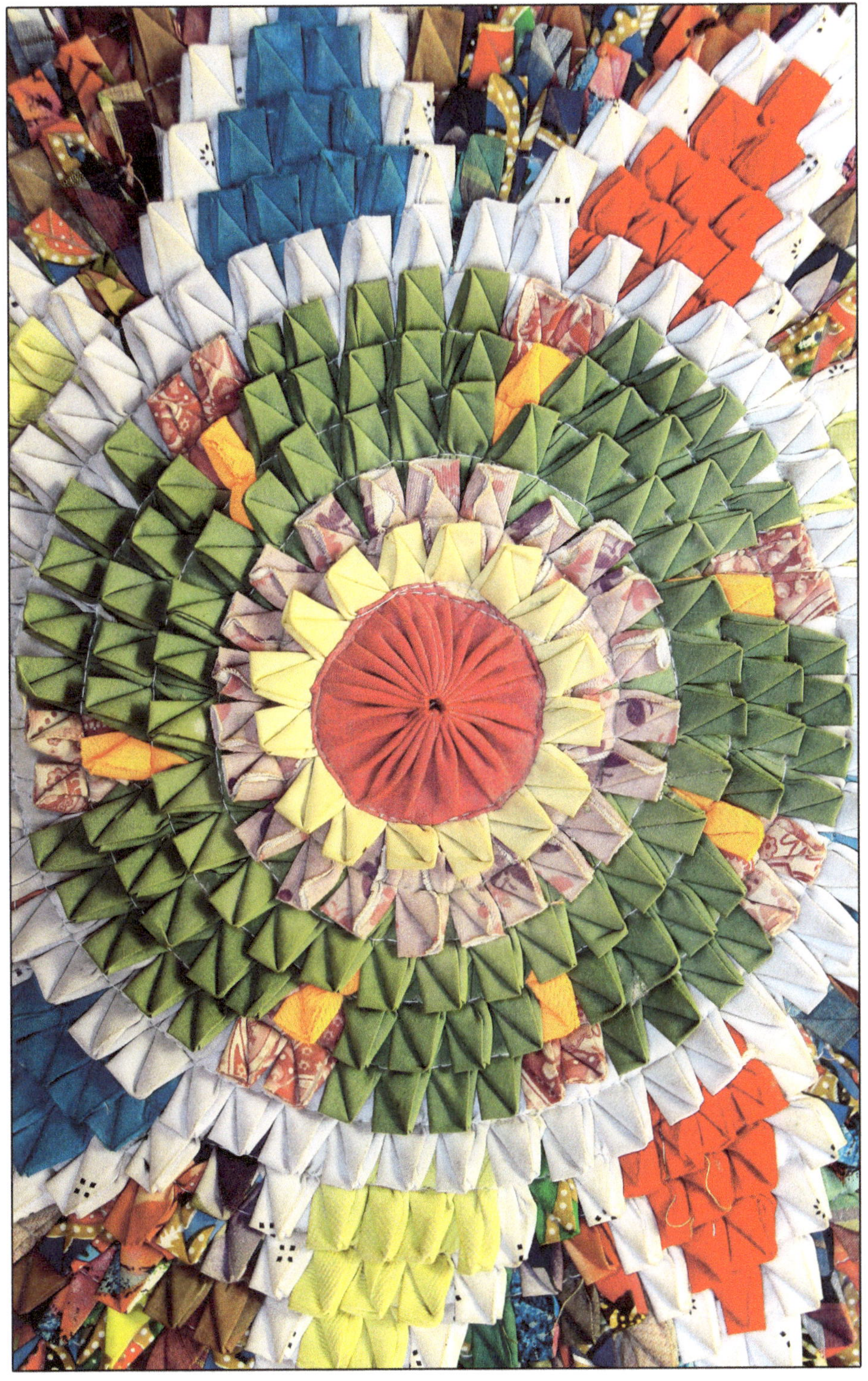

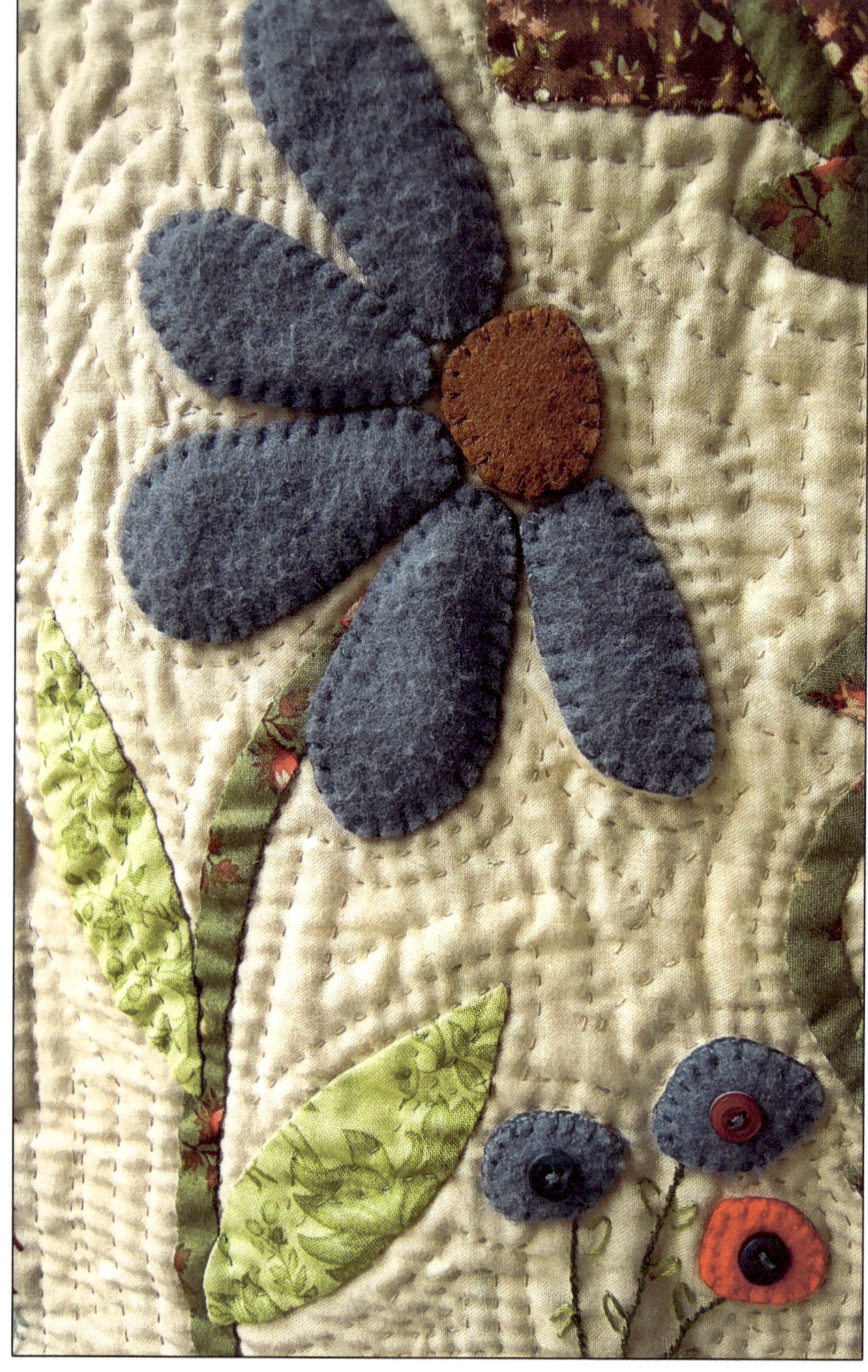

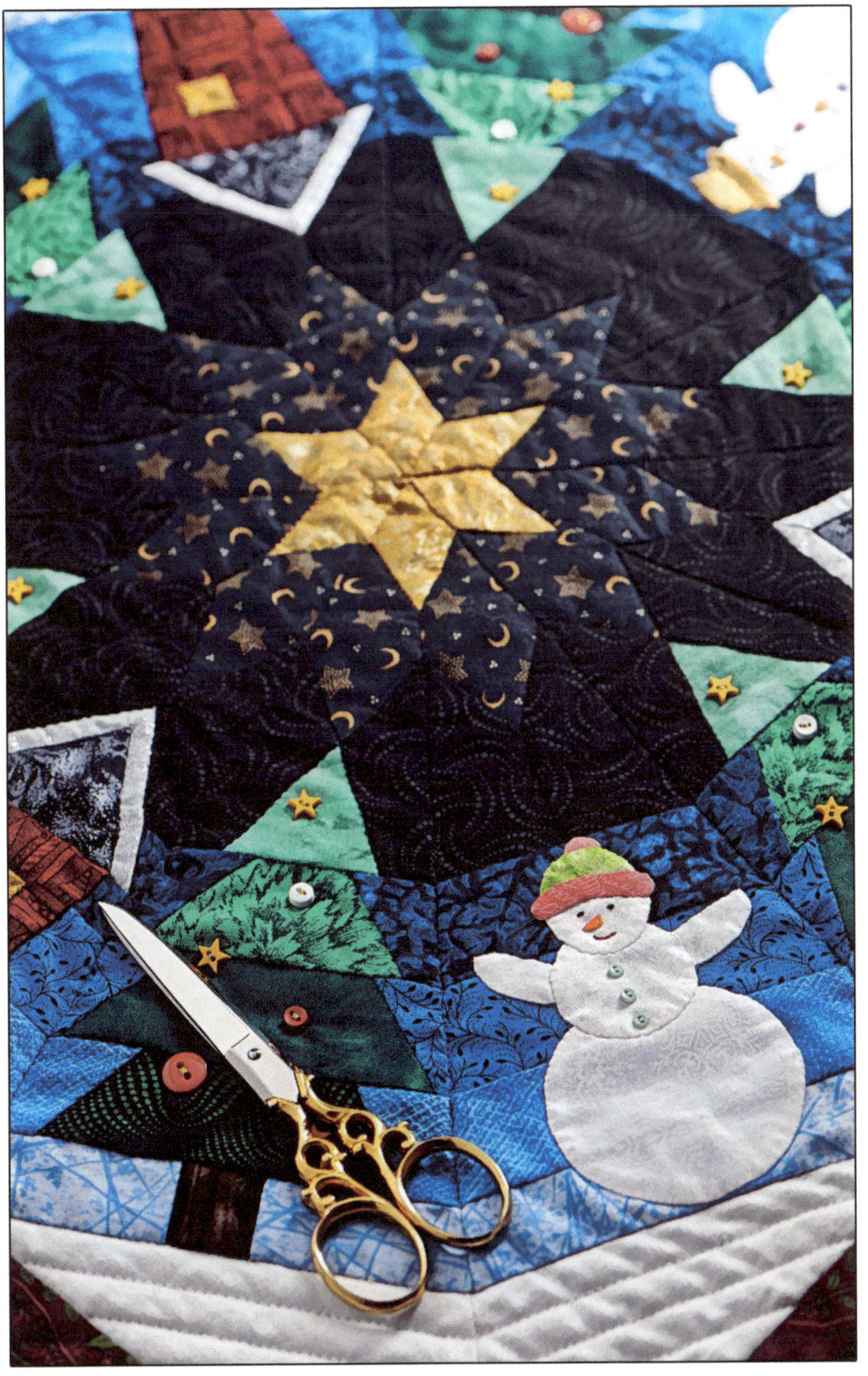

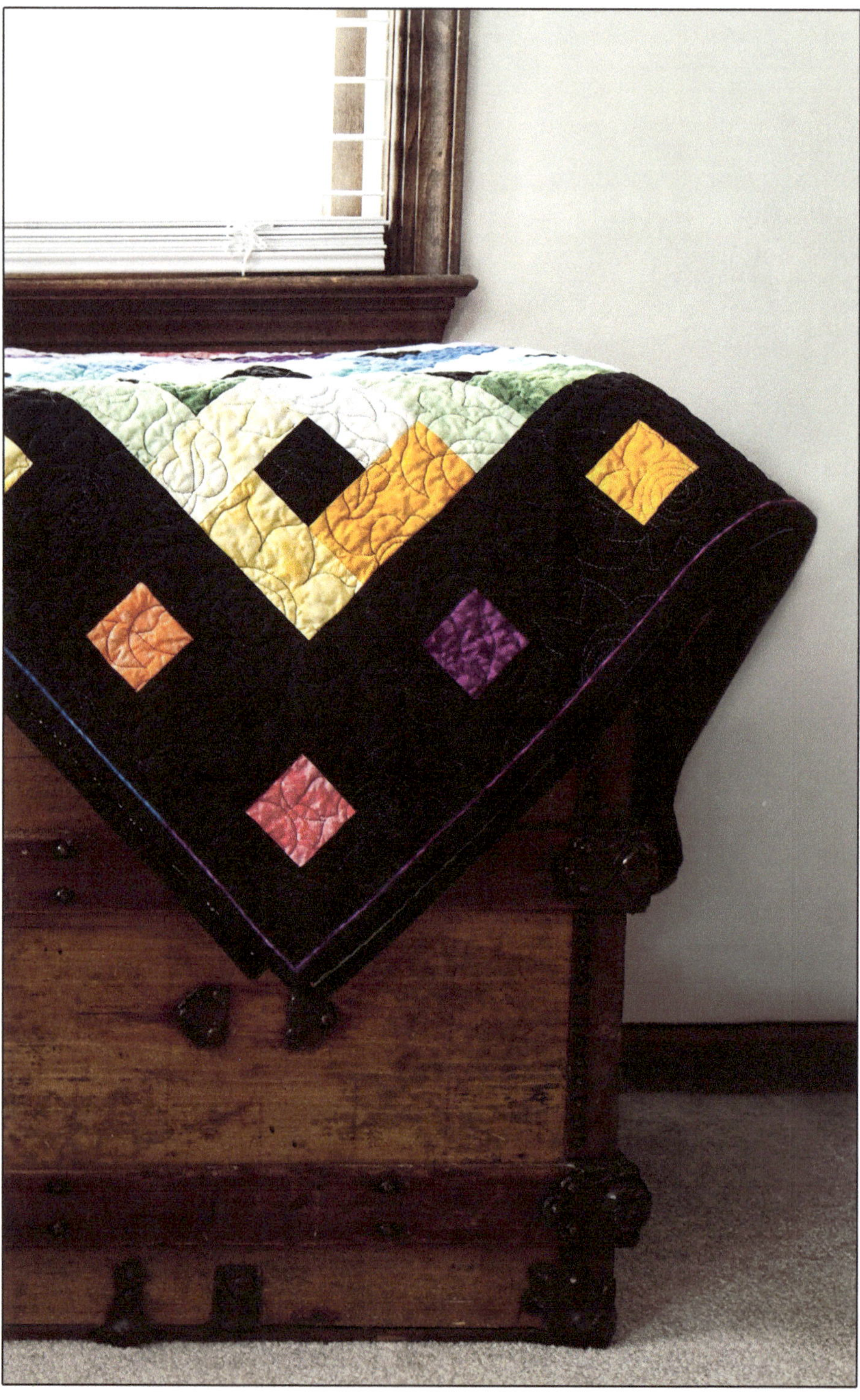

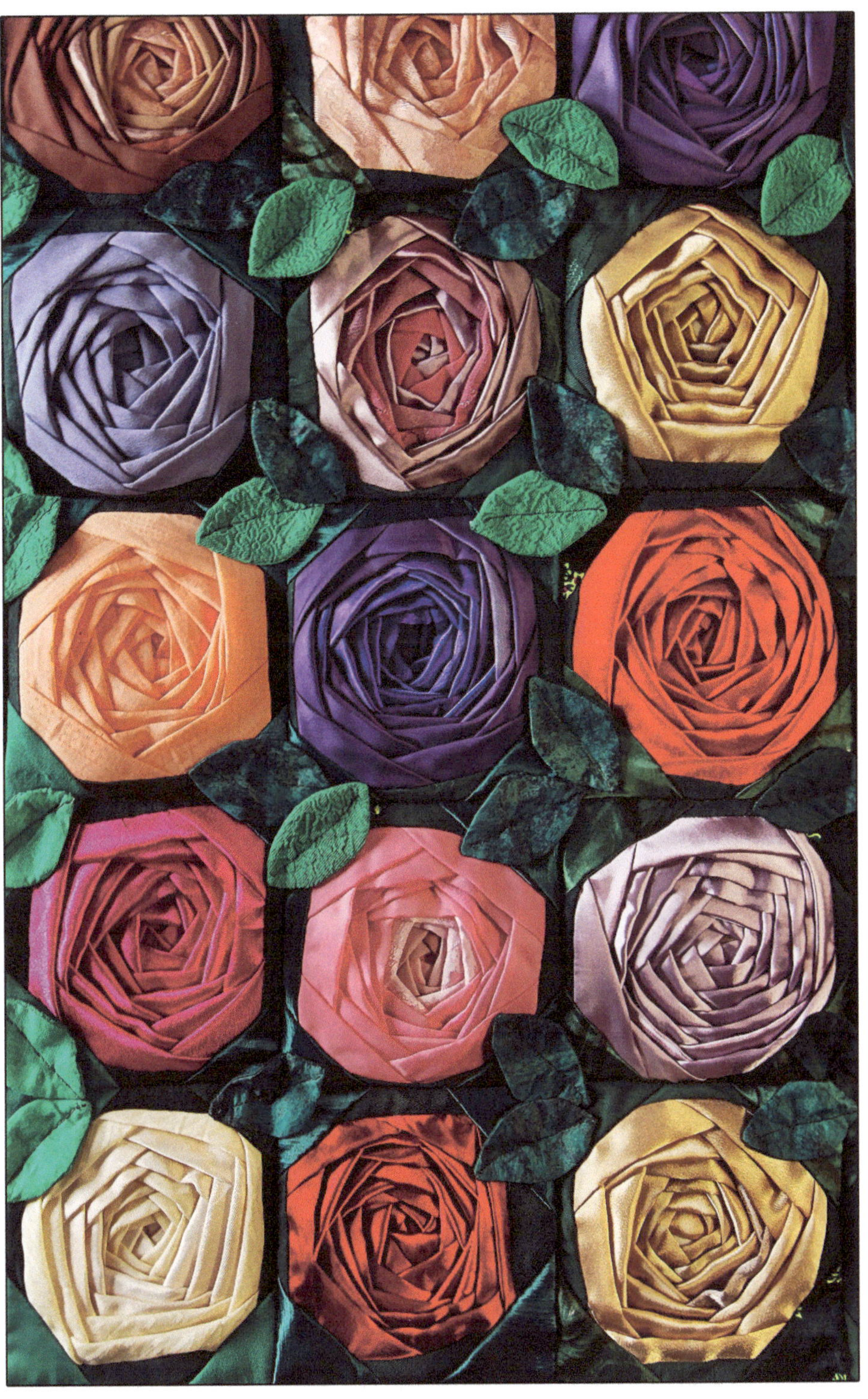

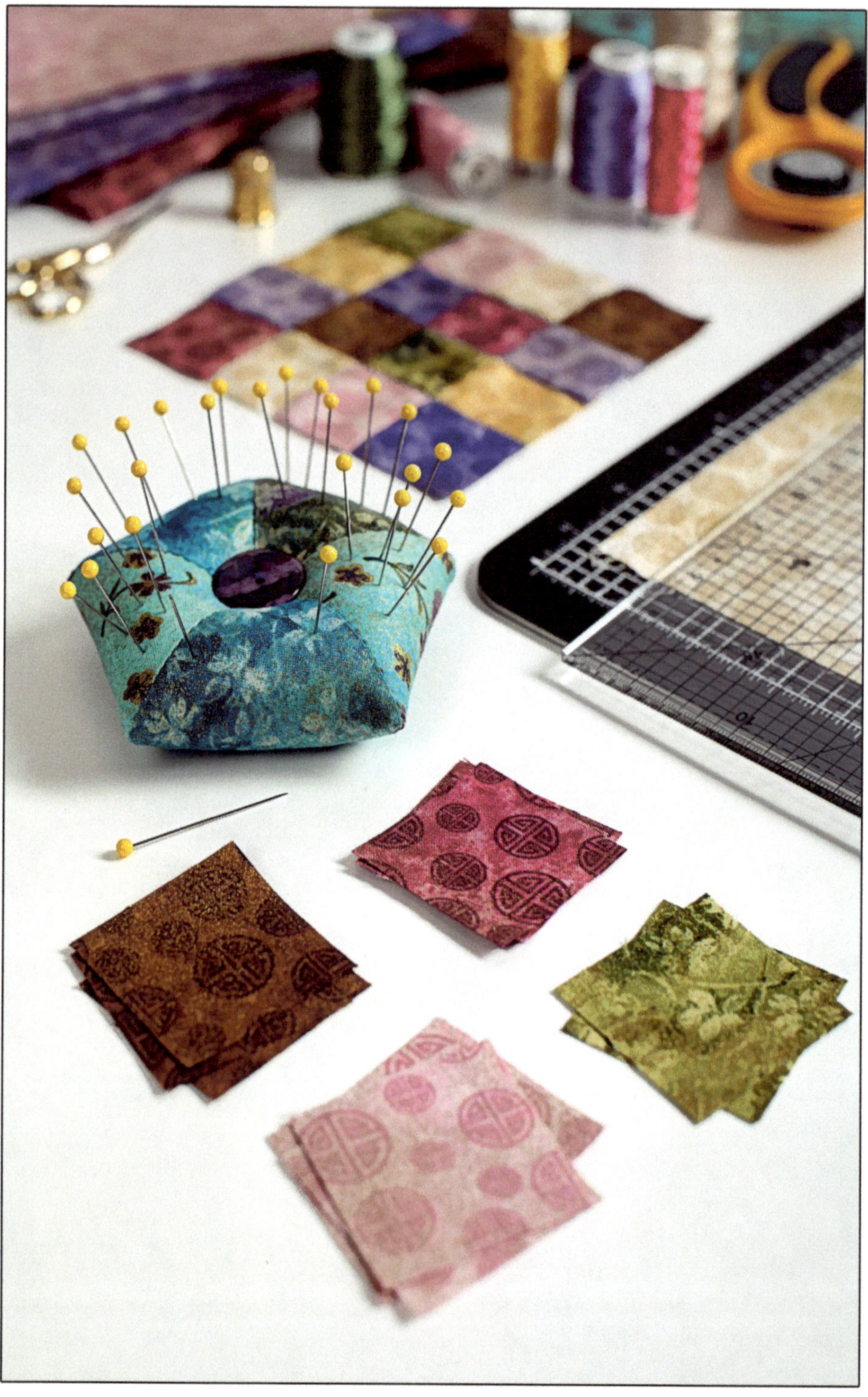

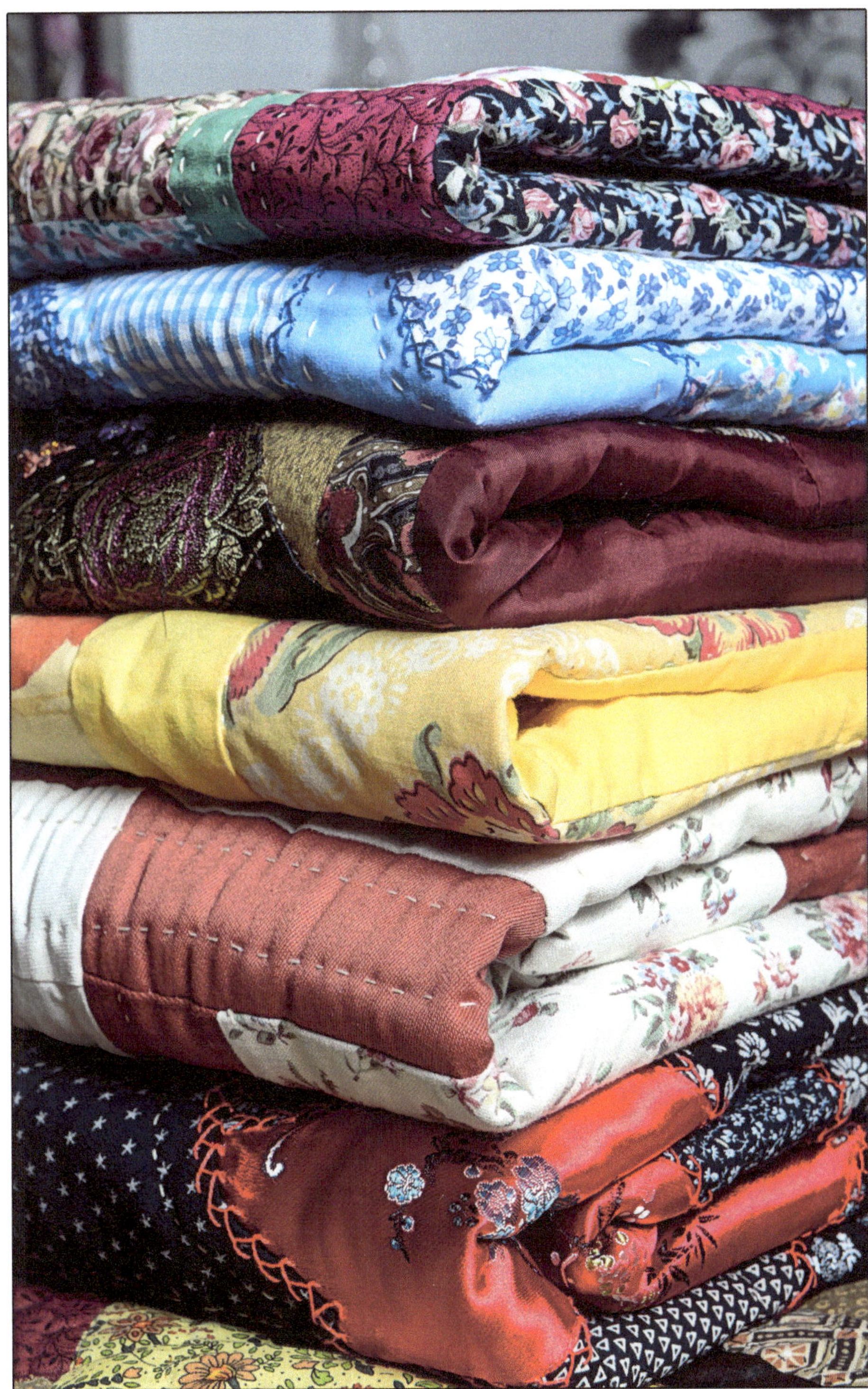

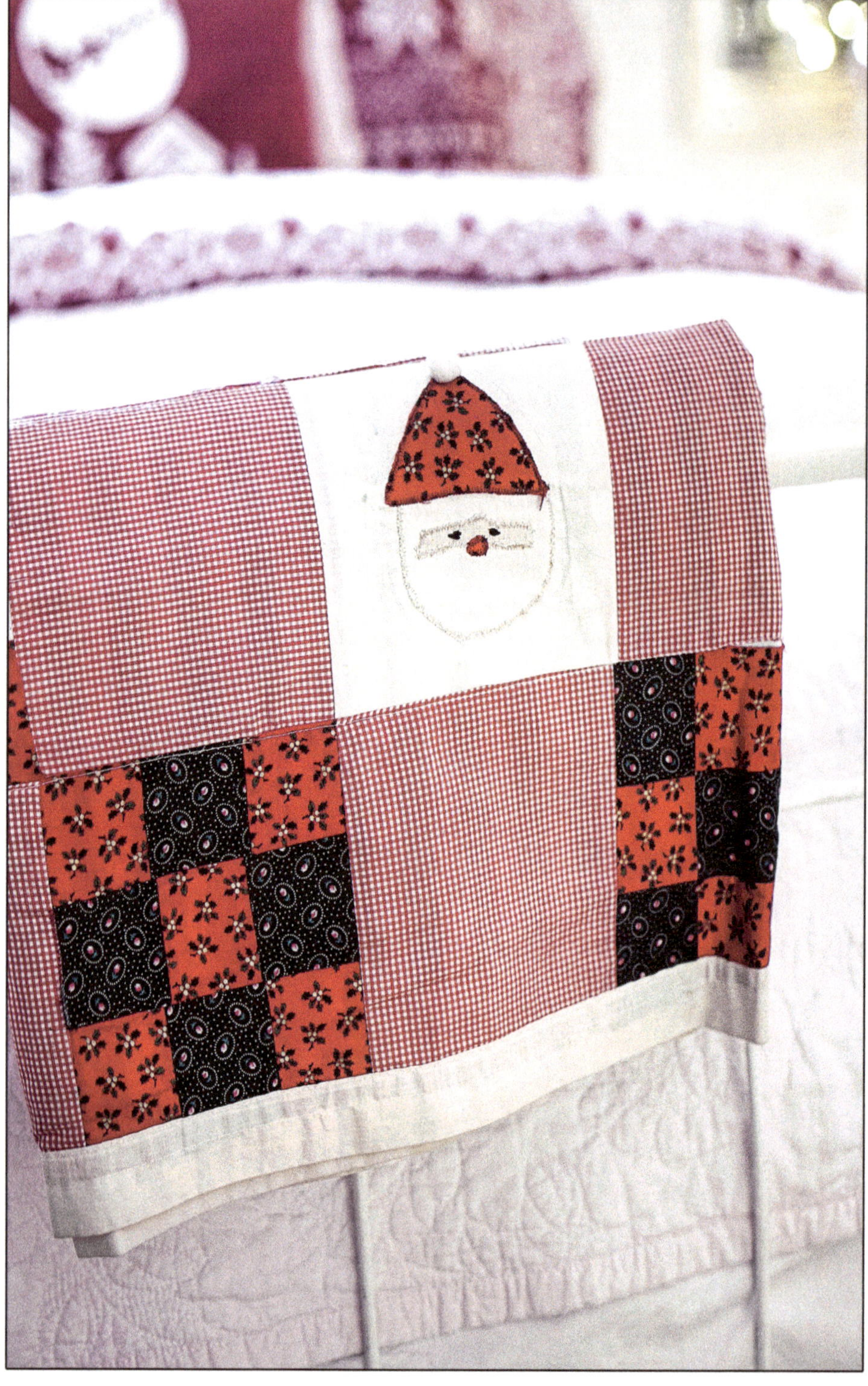

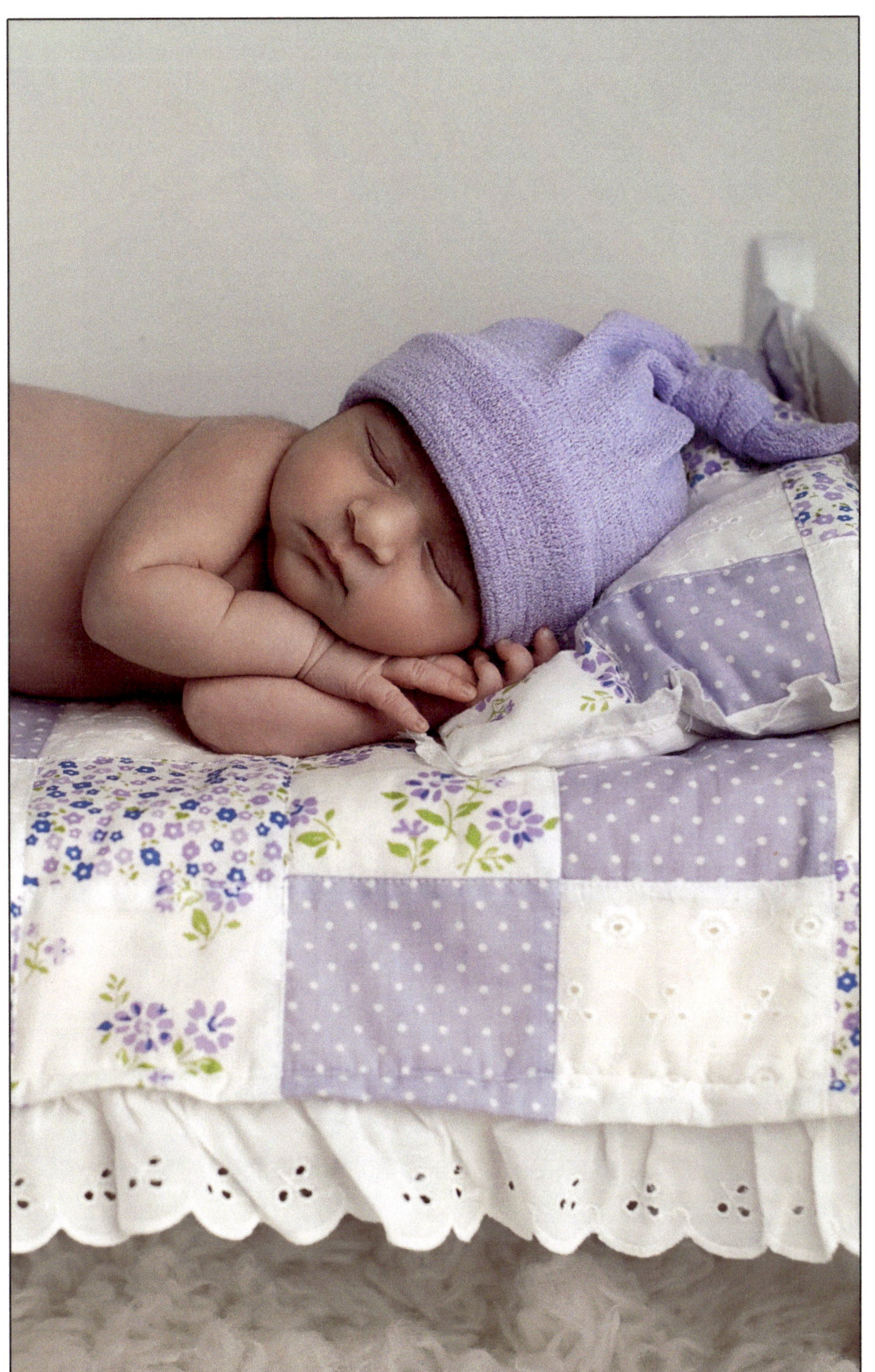

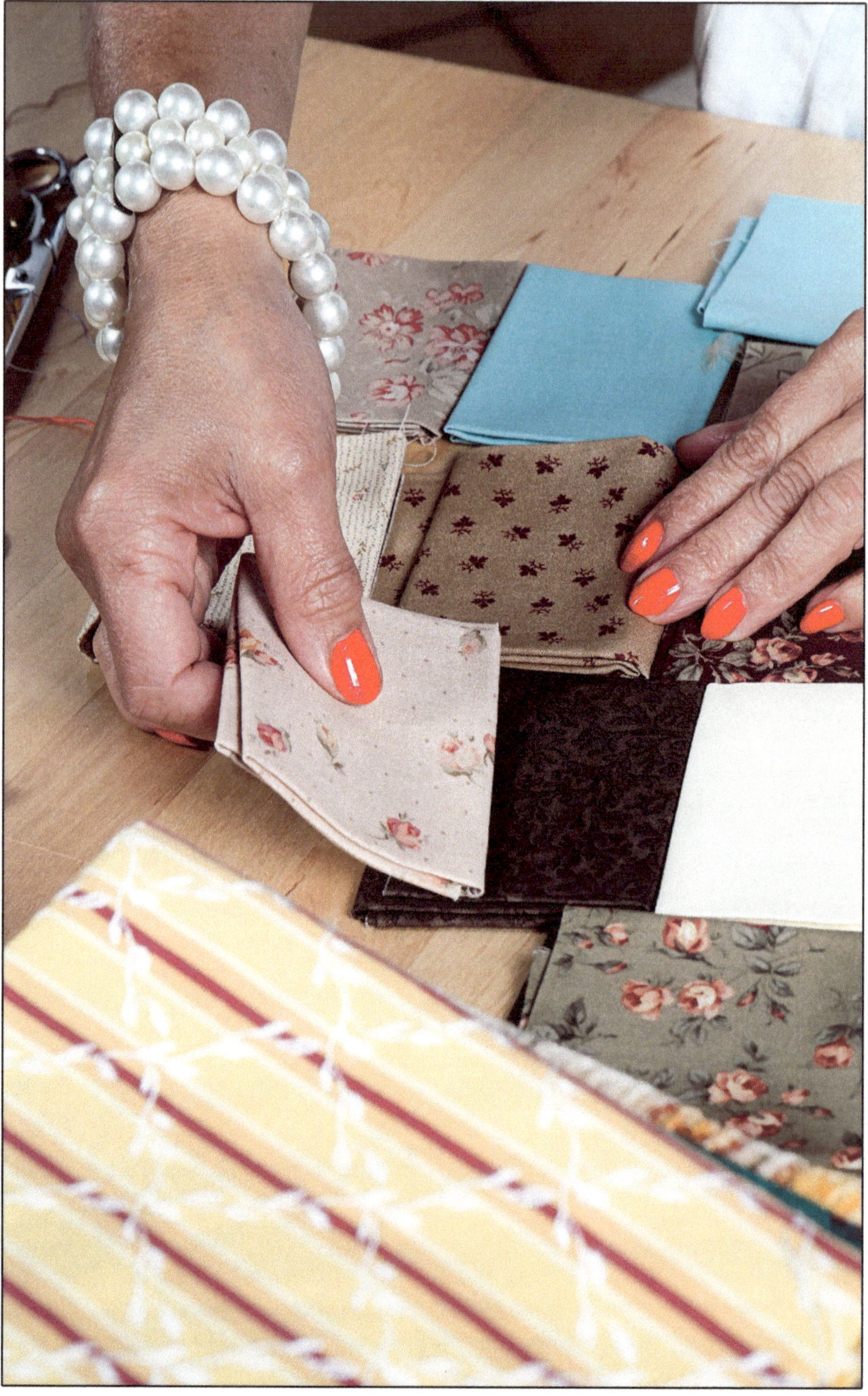

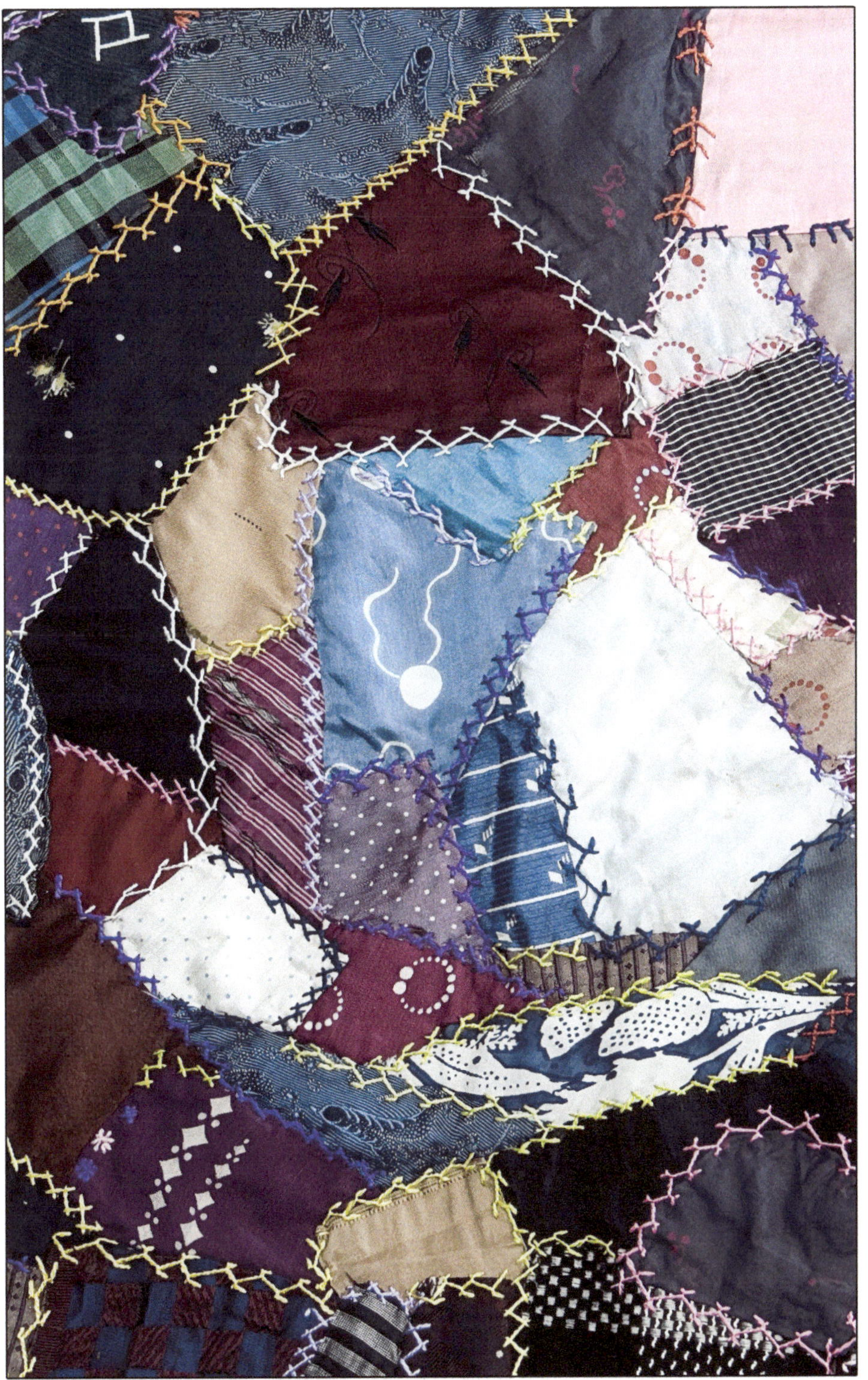

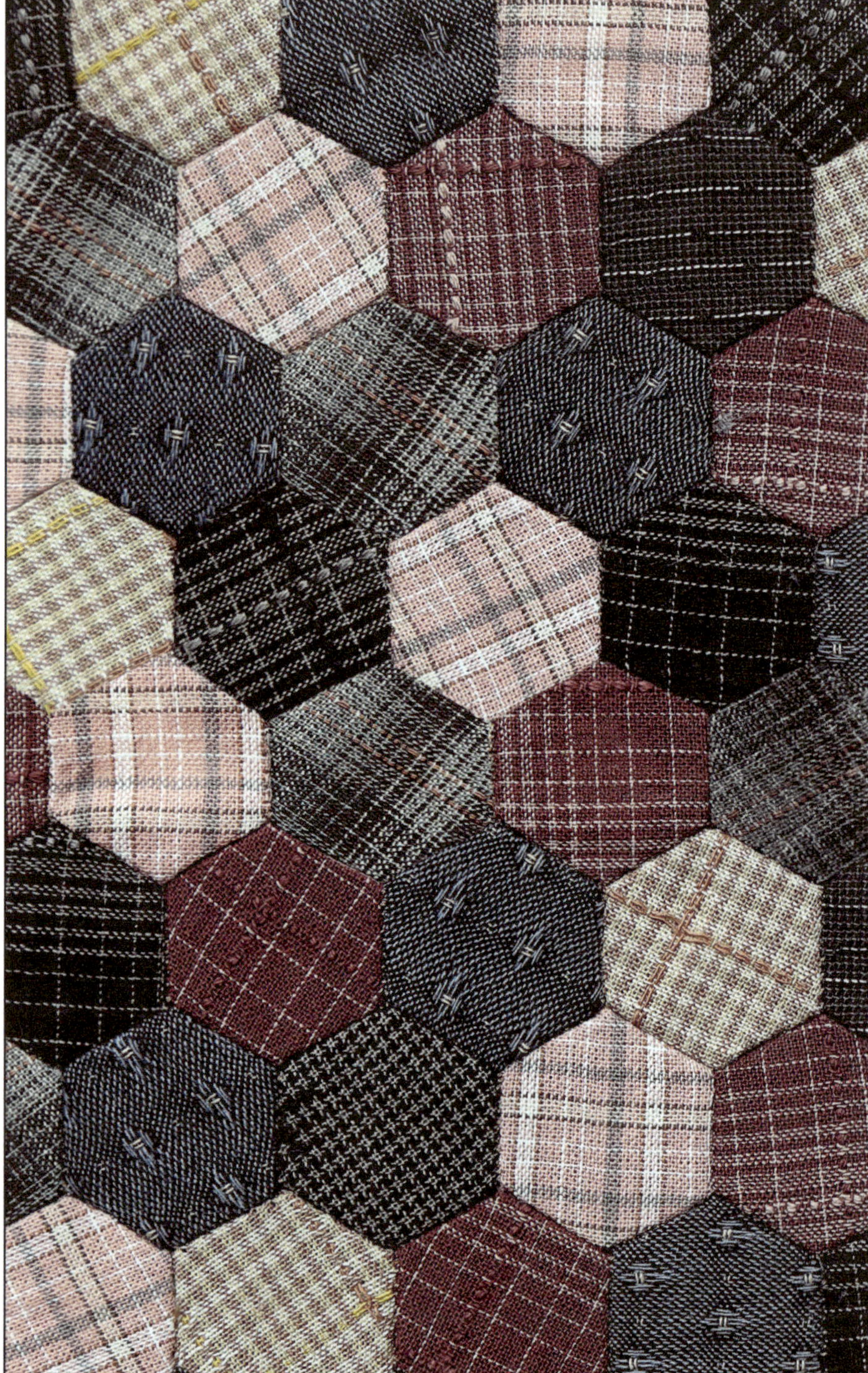

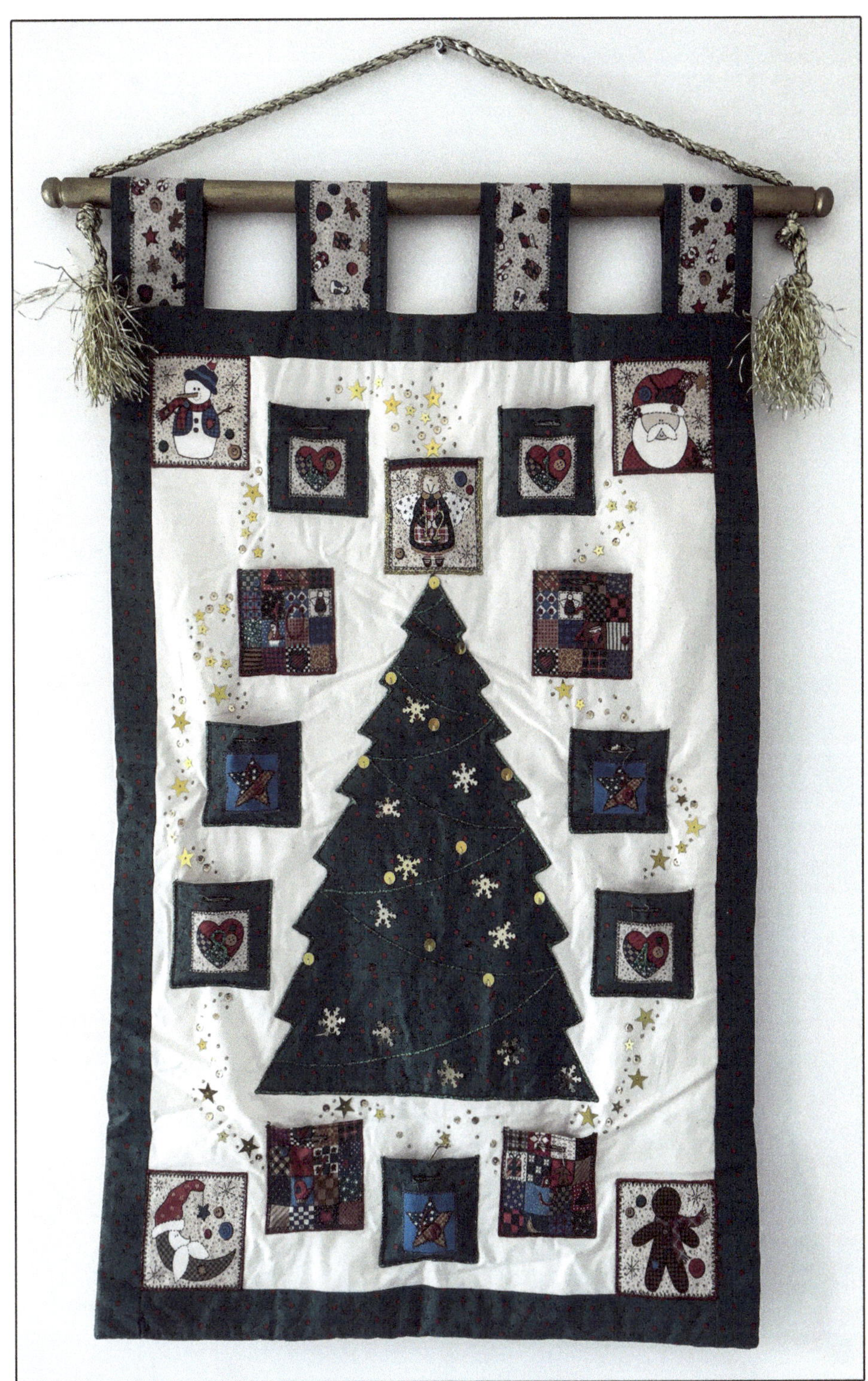